Transnational Media and Third World Development

**Recent Titles in
Contributions to the Study of
Mass Media and Communications**

News of Crime: Courts and Press in Conflict
J. Edward Gerald

As Good As Any: Foreign Correspondence on American Radio, 1930–1940
David H. Hosley

Freedom for the College Student Press: Court Cases and Related Decisions Defining the Campus Fourth Estate Boundaries
Louis E. Ingelhart

The Press and the Decline of Democracy: The Democratic Socialist Response in Public Policy
Robert G. Picard

Innovators and Preachers: The Role of the Editor in Victorian England
Joel H. Wiener, editor

Press Law and Press Freedom for High School Publications: Court Cases and Related Decisions Discussing Free Expression Guarantees and Limitations for High School Students and Journalists
Louis E. Ingelhart

Free Flow of Information: A New Paradigm
Achal Mehra

Shared Vulnerability: The Media and American Perceptions of the Bhopal Disaster
Lee Wilkins

Communications and History: Theories of Media, Knowledge, and Civilization
Paul Heyer

Oratorical Encounters: Selected Studies and Sources of Twentieth-Century Accusations and Apologies
Halford Ross Ryan, editor

Transnational Media and Third World Development

THE STRUCTURE AND IMPACT OF IMPERIALISM

William H. Meyer

CONTRIBUTIONS TO THE STUDY OF MASS MEDIA AND COMMUNICATIONS, NUMBER 11

Greenwood Press
NEW YORK • WESTPORT, CONNECTICUT • LONDON

Library of Congress Cataloging-in-Publication Data

Meyer, William H.
  Transnational media and Third World development : the structure and impact of imperialism / William H. Meyer.
  p. cm.—(Contributions to the study of mass media and communications, ISSN 0732-4456 ; no. 11)
  Bibliography: p.
  Includes index.
  ISBN 0-313-26264-0 (lib. bdg. : alk. paper)
  1. Communication—Developing countries. 2. Communication—International cooperation. 3. Communication, International. 4. Violence—Developing countries. 5. Communication in economic development. 6. Intercultural communication. I. Title. II. Series.
P92.2.M49 1988
001.51′09172′4—dc19   88-10239

British Library Cataloguing in Publication Data is available.

Copyright © 1988 by William H. Meyer

All rights reserved. No portion of this book may be reproduced, by any process or technique, without the express written consent of the publisher.

Library of Congress Catalog Card Number: 88-10239
ISBN: 0-313-26264-0
ISSN: 0732-4456

First published in 1988

Greenwood Press, Inc.
88 Post Road West, Westport, Connecticut 06881

Printed in the United States of America

The paper used in this book complies with the Permanent Paper Standard issued by the National Information Standards Organization (Z39.48-1984).

10 9 8 7 6 5 4 3 2 1

Copyright Acknowledgments

  Research for Chapter Three was funded in part by National Science Foundation grant #SES-8403811, and by a University of Delaware General Research Grant.

  Chapter Four is reprinted from *International Interactions* (1987), 13 (4).

  Chapter Five is reprinted from *Social Science Quarterly* (1988), 69 (1).

In memory of Benjamin A. Most,
edifying teacher and innovative scholar

Contents

Figures and Tables	ix
Abbreviations	xi
Preface	xiii
1. Introduction	1
2. Two Conceptions of "News"	17
3. Flows of News and Broadcasting to the Third World	41
4. International Communication and Cultural Imperialism	63
5. Communication and Domestic Violence in the Third World	95
6. International Relations Theory and Communication Policy	111
Bibliography	123
Index	129

Figures and Tables

FIGURES

3.1	The Neocolonial Structure of International News Flows	60
4.1	Initial Specification of the Structural Thesis	67
4.2	Further Specification of the Structural Thesis	68
4.3	Third Specification of the Cultural Imperialism Thesis	72
5.1	Specification of the Violence Thesis	102

TABLES

2.1	A Comparison of Three Press Institutions	31
3.1	The Flow of Broadcasting to the Third World	42
3.2	Average Broadcasting in Forty-three Developing Nations	43
3.3	Percentage of All News for International Reporting	48
3.4	Regions Covered in African and Latin American Presses	48
3.5	1,600 News Items According to Topics	49
3.6	Newswires Identified as Sources	50
3.7	Topics According to Source (Percentages)	52
3.8	Spot News Versus Developmental Reporting	53

3.9	Mean Values for Developmental Reports—Analysis of Variance (ANOVA)	54
3.10	Regions Covered According to Their Colonial History	56
3.11	News Flows as Compared with Imperial Hegemony	57
4.1	Coefficients for Equation [4.1]	74
4.2	Coefficients for Equation [4.1a]	75
4.3	Coefficients for Equation [4.1b]	77
4.4	Coefficients for Equation [4.1c]	79
4.5	Coefficients for Equation [4.1a]: Fourth World	80
4.6	Coefficients for Equation [4.1c]: Fourth World	81
4.7	Coefficients for Equation [4.2a]	82
4.8	Coefficients for Equation [4.2a]: Fourth World	83
4.9	Coefficients for Equation [4.3a]	84
4.10	Coefficients for Equation [4.3b]	85
5.1	Coefficients for Equation [5.1a]	103
5.2	Coefficients for Equation [5.1b]	105
5.3	Coefficients for Equation [5.1c]	105
5.4	Coefficients for Equation [5.2]	106
6.1	A Typology of Economic Development and Press Freedom	116
6.2	LDC Rankings According to Sovereignty and Stability	116

Abbreviations

ADV	Advertising Per Capita
AFP	Agence France Presse
AP	Associated Press
ASEAN	Association of Southeast Asian Nations
CONS	Consumer Goods as a Percentage of Total Imports
DBS	Direct Broadcast Satellite
ED	Ethnic Divisions
GINI	GINI Index of Landed Inequality
GNP	Gross National Product
ILET	Latin American Institute for Transnational Studies
IPDC	International Program for the Development of Communication
IPI	International Press Institute
IR	International Relations
LDC	Less Developed Country
LUX	Luxury Items Imported
MI	Media Imported
MNC	Multinational Corporation
NIEO	New International Economic Order
NWIO	New World Information Order
NYAP	New York Associated Press
OECD	Organization for Economic Cooperation and Development

OPEC	Organization of Petroleum Exporting Countries
PF	Press Freedom
SOP	Standard Operating Procedure
TASS	Telegraph Agency of the Soviet Union
TNNA	Transnational News Agency
Unesco	United Nations Educational, Scientific, and Cultural Organization
Unicef	United Nations International Children's Emergency Fund
UPA	United Press Association
UPI	United Press International

Preface

This book tells a story of the New World Information Order (NWIO). It is the story of the origin, development, theoretical foundation, validity, and future prospects of a major international reform movement. To adequately tell the tale of the NWIO, however, requires that we attend to much more than just these areas. The tale of the NWIO is actually a story of many stories. The story of the NWIO is a story of communication, culture, and crises.

To tell the story of global communication is to discuss the topics of international news reporting, interstate information flows, communication in the service of national development, and the structure of international relations. To tell the story of contemporary transnational cultural trends requires a consideration of cultural exchanges between the North and the South, intercultural communication as a function of the advantages enjoyed by the North over the South, and, especially, the effects of Western forms of communication on the ways of life in non-Western societies. Telling a tale of the crises which helped to evoke the NWIO movement is to speak of crises at several levels. There is the "crisis *in* international news" and there is the "crisis nature *of* international news." There are even those who would argue that international news and information flows serve as a major source for many of the current crises in Third World politics (i.e., political instability in developing nations as a result of inputs of information coming from the West).

The research presented here sorts through this plethora of issues by starting from the NWIO platform itself, moving on to the doctrines which support these policies, and then evaluating the doctrines empirically to assess the advisability of NWIO recommendations. In my own personal journey through these matters, I have been aided by many people. I would like to thank Vernon Van Dyke, who allowed me access to his personal files on the politics of international communication. Special thanks must also go to Jean Meyer, the late Benjamin A. Most, and John S. Nelson for their useful comments on earlier drafts of this work.

Transnational Media and Third World Development

1

Introduction

For over a decade a series of debates in the General Assembly and other United Nations organs has revolved around the international systems of economics and technology. In 1974, nonaligned nations advanced a demand for a New International Economic Order (NIEO) during a special session of the General Assembly. An ongoing dialogue between North and South has focused since that time on imbalances in international relations that allegedly enrich the North and perpetuate dependency for the South. As a corollary to this concern for economic inequities, the Third World nations quickly broadened their demands in 1976 to include a New World Information Order (NWIO). The NWIO was meant to be a device for balancing international inequalities in the flows of information, news, and communication technologies.

In late 1977, the International Commission for the Study of Communication Problems (or the MacBride Commission) began its highly controversial work. The MacBride Commission was established by the United Nations Educational, Scientific, and Cultural Organization (Unesco) to review "the totality of the problems of communication in modern society" and to suggest ways that a more just and effective international system of communication might be fostered. The Commission published a 1978 Interim Report and a Final Report in 1980. The discussions and reports generated by the Commission focused international debate upon particular characteristics of the international communication system. The proceedings of the MacBride Commission also intensified some of the hostilities on both sides (North and South) of these debates. The Reagan Administration, to show its displeasure with the NWIO, withdrew from Unesco in 1985 (see Chapter Four for a full listing of the Administration's charges against Unesco and its directors).

Since the inception of the NWIO debate, the government of the United States has been a leader of the faction which defends the status quo in international communication. American policies have tended to address short-term problems and suffer from a lack of long-range comprehensive planning. By concentrating on crisis-oriented planning for the next round of international meetings, American positions have appeared to the rest of the world as generally defensive and insensitive (Joyner and Lawson, 1986: 68; Richstad and Anderson, 1981: 417). The American position has been to defend a free market in international news and communication as the best possible system (U.S. Department of State, 1981: 78–80; and 1982: 66–70). Recurrent attacks on this position by the Third World were met by the Reagan Administration's often repeated threat to pull out of Unesco, a threat the United States made good on in January of 1985 (see Coate, 1988).

Due to the nature of the many problems addressed but left unresolved by the MacBride Commission, issues involving international communication will continue to be central to many of the debates and conflicts in international relations. The West in general and the United States in particular often suffer from their lack of information in regard to the true nature of events in much of the world. That portion of Western newspapers which is devoted to international news is steadily shrinking (McPhail, 1987: 14). Ironically, and at the same time, the centers of East-West conflicts are shifting from North Atlantic to Third World contexts (e.g., Afghanistan, Central America, southern Africa). Reliance by the West upon energy supplies and strategic minerals located in the Third World also remains high and, in some cases, is increasing. Information to the West about the Third World is in danger of being reduced (and, in some cases, cut off entirely) due to tensions over the international system of communication. Western intransigence over possible reforms in the international communication network threatens to curtail information from these areas just at a time when we need to know more about the Third World to protect vital national interests.

Given the increased strategic importance of developments in the Third World, Western neglect and complacency regarding the international information system are indeed perilous. Western foreign correspondents have been subjected to increasingly open forms of manipulation by some non-Western powers (as was the case during the 1979–1981 Iranian crisis) (Richstad and Anderson, 1981: 409). Developing countries lack the communication resources necessary for integrating and representing their interests effectively (Mowlana, 1986: 100). This disadvantaged position causes nonaligned states to politicize international negotiations and adopt obstructionist stances (O'Brien and Helleniner, 1980: 456). These conditions often make future bargaining impossible and jeopardize past gains (as was the case at the recent Law of the Seas Conference). Western disregard and inaction with respect to Third World charges may force those nations to act unilaterally and close off media access to trouble spots and strategic areas. Problems with lack of information and ineffective Western foreign policies would then necessarily increase.

Beyond the considerations of helping to protect national interests by ensuring the continued flow of international communication, there is a need for new research into information flows that can contribute to an understanding of other topics of interest to international scholars and national policymakers. It is often assumed that the current international system is one characterized by geopolitical spheres of influence. One might ask if there are also such things as "informational spheres of influence." That is, can one nation persuade or compel another to bring its foreign and domestic policies into "compliance" through the manipulation and control of international news and information? If they are identifiable, do such informational spheres of influence follow the old patterns of colonial domination? If we are living in an "information age" as some observers have argued, is the control of international information flows a more effective way to generate compliance than (say) political or military pressure?

New research into international communication should also shed light on the political and economic difficulties experienced by the "late-late" developing nations of the Third World. To what extent might the problems of underdevelopment and instability experienced by those nations be attributable to the nature of the international informational system? If the long time span over which the West developed contributed to the relative stability of Western nations, and if this same process has been collapsed into a much shorter time-frame for late-late developers, then are the problems of accelerated and inconstant development exacerbated by an international "demonstration effect," an effect allegedly promoted via global communications?

These considerations make it in the best interests of the United States to be avidly concerned with claims made by nonaligned nations concerning our communication policies. It is necessary to pursue acceptable forms of accommodation of interests as quickly as possible. Beyond our own self-interest, it is also incumbent upon the United States as a major world power to review carefully the claims of the Third World regarding "cultural imperialism" and information inequities. Further study is required to see which (if any) of these charges are justified, and, if so, how we might promote international cooperation to redress some of these grievances.

THE "NEW ORDERS" IN INTERNATIONAL RELATIONS

During the decades of the 1950s and 1960s, the rise of nationalism and the end of colonialism spread throughout most of the Third World. Many less developed countries (LDCs) gained political independence at this time, but their national autonomy continued to be compromised through other means. Most LDCs remained begrudgingly dependent on the former imperial states for trade, technology, expertise, and cultural resources. The pride and excitement generated by newly won political sovereignty were quickly displaced by disillusionment and resentment.

This sense of dissatisfaction with the structure of international relations was combined with a perception in the Third World that Western powers were doing little or nothing to aid LDCs in their quest for economic and cultural autonomy. Given their sheer weight in numbers and their majority in the General Assembly, the Group of Seventy-seven (LDCs) felt confident in turning to the United Nations as its means for a restructuring of global affairs. Developing nations were also enouraged by a show of strength from OPEC (the Organization of Petroleum Exporting Countries) during the 1973 oil embargo. If political muscle could be gained through economic cartels (for commodities other than oil), OPEC's success would be duplicated by fellow Third World nations.

The proposal for an NIEO was the first global design by LDCs for breaking their dependence on Western trade and Western technologies. The NIEO platform addressed four key areas:

1. LDCs were to be given absolute sovereignty over their natural resources, including the right of nationalization.
2. Preferential treatment was to be given to Third World goods in Western markets. LDCs were to be given better access to those markets. Prices for Third World goods were to be increased and then linked (indexed) to future rises in the prices of goods imported into the LDCs. Producer cartels were also encouraged.
3. Grants, gifts, and other transfers of advanced technologies from the West to the Third World were to be vastly increased and funded by the wealthy industrialized nations.
4. Finally, new controls were to be placed on multinational corporations (MNCs) which operate in the Third World (see Weston et al., 1980: 278–283).

These measures were designed to promote more rapid development in the Third World, while simultaneously reducing the dependency of the LDCs on the West.

The campaign for the NWIO followed quickly on the heels of the NIEO. Many difficulties arise within the political economy of an LDC that relies on foreign sources for news and communication technologies. These problems parallel difficulties that LDCs have previously encountered while relying on Western modes of modernization in other areas, prior difficulties the NIEO was designed to alleviate. The technology necessary for modernizing a national news agency or broadcasting studio is primarily a Western export. It is controlled by MNCs. It is capital-intensive rather than labor-intensive. Furthermore, developing countries find that they must rely on foreign sources of capital to obtain this hardware, and their choices are generally determined by foreign tastes (MacBride Commission, 1981a: 55). These are technologies, therefore, that tend to reduce the self-reliance and national autonomy of LDCs. Unesco has warned that countries dependent on aid to finance purchases of new communication systems "may find themselves committed to the installation of equipment from a donor country which proves inappropriate in technical design or standards" (Sommerlad, 1975: 30).

In light of these facts, Third World leaders perceived the need for a new order in international communication as well as in international economics. The NWIO platform can be seen in large part as the NIEO applied to communication. Four key provisions of the NWIO are as follows:

1. Absolute sovereignty for LDCs over all of their "informational resources"
2. Preferential treatment for Third World *news* in Western markets. The percentage of news about LDCs was to be increased in the Western press. "Horizontal communication" (that which is exchanged between LDCs) was to be promoted and "vertical communication" (that which is exchanged between developed and developing nations) was to become less pervasive
3. Direct grants and other gifts of advanced communication technologies from the West to the Third World
4. The breakup of the Western transnational news agencies (TNNAs: Agence France Presse, Associated Press, Reuters, and United Press International). These MNCs of communication were to be closely regulated when operating within Third World nations (see MacBride Commission, 1981b).

At different times, NWIO supporters have presented it as a prerequisite to the NIEO; or as an integral component of the NIEO, and/or as a tool to aid in the creation of the NIEO. Mustapha Masmoudi, Tunisia's permanent delegate to Unesco and a former Minister of Information, is a leading advocate of the NWIO. When writing on the "aims of the NWIO" Masmoudi has argued that, in regard to the Third World, the new order requires the training of news professionals in a manner that inculcates "the values of the new international economic order" (1981: 87). In regard to international organizations, one aim of the NWIO would be "helping to formulate research programs and to establish training centers so as to enable developing countries to produce radio and television programs designed to serve the aims of the New International Economic Order"(1981: 90). Masmoudi goes on to argue that one primary reason for the lack of success in prior efforts to establish the NIEO is that "certain media . . . have frequently sought to make a mockery of the principles advocated by the Third World, when they have not simply ignored them." Therefore, "the establishment of a new world information order" which would allow the Third World viewpoint to be more widely and fairly heard in the West "must be considered as the essential corollary of the new international economic order" (1981: 96).

Even Leonard Sussman, executive director of the Freedom House research foundation and a leading opponent of the NWIO, has acknowledged the fact that the NIEO would be impossible to achieve without increases in flows of information between developed and developing nations. "A new international economic order can hardly develop without dependable, verifiable information about many aspects of a country's social, political and economic development." Sussman also agrees that it is in the West's own best interests to increase inputs of information from the less developed world. "Many of the international crises originate there.... And, it must be admitted, we all need to know much more about the realities of the Third World" (1981b: 349–350).

The MacBride Commission also spoke of the relationship between the NIEO and the NWIO when presenting its Final Report to the Twenty-first General Conference of Unesco in Belgrade, in 1981. Recommendation sixty-eight (of eighty-two) is as follows:

The close relationship between the establishment of a new international economic order and the new world information order should be carefully considered by the technical bodies dealing with these issues. Concrete plans of action linking both processes should be implemented within the United Nations system. The United Nations, in approving the international development strategy, should consider the communications sector as an integral element of it and not merely as an instrument of public information. (1981b: 397)

The Declaration on the Establishment of a New International Economic Order was quickly followed by the adoption of the Programme of Action on the Establishment of a New International Economic Order. In a similar fashion, Unesco's Final Report on the NWIO was quickly followed by the establishment of the International Program for the Development of Communication (IPDC). The IPDC was designed to "serve as the mechanism through which financial and technical assistance might be channeled to developing countries to help improve their communication capabilities" (Richstad and Anderson, 1981: 3; see also McPhail, 1987: 218–228; and Sidel, 1984).

THREE SCHOOLS OF THOUGHT ON INTERNATIONAL COMMUNICATION

Positions taken by journalists, diplomats, and academicians concerning international communication have cut across economic, regional, and national boundaries. However, three major schools of thought can be identified. These three camps all agree that international imbalances exist in information flows and technology transfers. What separates the three camps are their stances on the sources of the imbalances, the effects that they believe media to have on societies (particularly underdeveloped societies), and the extent to which they would go in altering the current international order. The policy proposals from each group, therefore, differ accordingly, particularly their positions on government controls over media versus a free press.

The Conservatives

The first major school of thought consists of the conservatives. Because this camp has received the backing of the U.S. government, it is politically the most powerful group (although not necessarily the largest). The conservative American viewpoint was strongly represented on the MacBride Commission by Ambassador Elie Abel, and has been frequently articulated in State Department bulletins. The conservative cause has also been forcefully defended by Sussman.

The conservatives deny that imbalances in international information flows are due to the activities of governments and media in the West (U.S. Department of State, 1982: 67). They see imbalances in news flows as being caused by certain "natural" characteristics of information gathering and dissemination. According to John C. Merrill, director of the School of Journalism at Louisiana State University, "unevenness of flow is a basic characteristic of news—and not only of news flow, but of water flow, oil flow, money flow, population flow, and food flow" (1981: 156).

The conservatives also deny charges that a free market of information and a free press have adverse effects on underdeveloped nations. In a comment on the Final Report of the MacBride Commission, Abel states: "At no time has the commission seen evidence adduced in support of the notion that market and commercial considerations necessarily exert a negative effect [upon societies]" (MacBride Commission, 1981b: 388). The conservatives prefer to stress the positive aspects of a free market in news and information, and point to Daniel Lerner's research from the Middle East to support their position. Lerner concluded that Western technology and Western newswires serve as tools of development for the Third World. These Western inputs, according to Lerner's theory, serve to overcome traditional (anti-modern) values, increase media exposure and literacy, and thus facilitate increased economic productivity and political participation (1964: 43–75; see the discussion of the Lerner thesis in Chapter Two).

Conservatives defend the status quo in international communication and argue against governmental control of the mass media. Sussman sees no middle ground or room for compromise on this central issue. He argues that there are only two choices open; either a Soviet form of press censorship and government controls, or the American tradition of press freedom (1981b: 348). The conservatives further defend Western styles of advertising (a target of the LDCs in the Final Report) as a necessary part of a free and independent press (U.S. Department of State, 1982: 66; see also Able's comment in Richstad and Anderson, 1981: 395). The principal assertion of the conservatives is that the dangers inherent in any form of media control are far greater than the possible pernicious effects of a free press.

Policy proposals from the conservatives consist primarily of platitudes about the need for a "free flow" of information. U.S. government policy "has relied on the premise that international acceptance of the moral principle of free flow of information should be the basis for the resolution of information issues of every kind" (Spero, 1982: 149). Because the United States has offered no practical responses to the problems caused by informational imbalances, Joan Spero charges that the United States remains "without an effective policy." The conservatives, led by the United States, have merely called for a strengthening of the free press—and vigorously attacked any argument in favor of governmental controls—while offering a single principle, the free flow, as a blanket solution to all information and media problems. The only recommendations of the MacBride Commission that the conservatives do favor are those which they feel can be directed against the Soviet bloc. These are the proposals that call for increases in media access to all opinions and those that condemn censorship by state officials.

The Reformists

A second school of thought is populated by reformists. This group receives much broader international support than the conservatives. Many Western journalists and media executives are also sympathetic to the reformists' arguments. Perhaps the most prominent international spokesman for the reformists is Sean MacBride of Ireland, president of the MacBride Commission.

Unlike the conservatives, the reformists readily admit that imbalances in information flows are due to the West's near-monopoly of newswires and technology. Reformists also recognize the harmful social and political affects that can result from the unregulated actions of Western TNNAs. However, the reformists believe that the current international order can be made more effective and equitable through a series of incremental adjustments. They do not go so far as to call for a fundamental restructuring of the international system. Reformists believe that much can be accomplished within the context of the current order, such as a reduction in the costs of communication for LDCs (i.e., lower newsprint costs), Western assistance to train journalists from LDCs, and increased coverage of Third World nations in the Western press.

The policy proposals of the reformists go much further than those offered by the conservatives in calling for new forms of international communication. In addition to increased coverage of the Third World, reformists advocate more coverage of ongoing projects for social, political, and economic development. Such "developmental journalism" would supplement or partially replace "spot news" which concentrates on episodic events such as riots, coups, and disasters (see Chapter Two for a full description of these two conceptions of news). To offset the imbalance in news flows, reformists have proposed that all nations uphold a right to communicate. The right to communicate would require more "true communication . . . a horizontal, interactive flow, a process of give and take" (d'Arcy, 1981: 122). Third World nations would prefer a more interactive, two-way form of communication, and less of the one-way flow that reflects the Western mass media mentality. The right to communicate would be facilitated, in part, by creating regional training centers in the South.

At the national level, the MacBride Commission (vanguard of the reformists) recommended that national news agencies be established in the forty LDCs currently lacking one, and that foreign correspondents be given access to all views, including "unofficial as well as official sources of information" (1981b: 391). The latter is a point on which the reformists and free press conservatives agree. However, the Commission did not go so far as to push for licensing journalists, or creating a code of journalistic ethics, or demanding a right of reply (i.e., giving poor countries the right to demand "equal time" in foreign presses when they think that they have received biased coverage). Such matters were put aside for later discussion. The campaign to license journalists, although garnering the greatest media attention of all NWIO issues, was later dropped by Unesco.

Reformists on the MacBride Commission called for a mix of governmental controls and free press institutions, a mix that would be determined on a nation-by-nation basis. Developing countries would be allowed a wide latitude in deciding just what combination of regulations and independent media would best suit their national goals. The Commission explicitly rejected the notion that any single broad principle (such as the free flow of information) should be ascribed overriding importance in all cases. Instead of "universal application of preconceived models" they prefer an admixture of policies to be defined on a case-by-case basis. The term used most often for this contextually defined blend of media policies and government programs is a "free and balanced flow."

The Structuralists

A third school of thought is also well represented in the literature on international communication. These are the structuralists. The structuralists include neo-Marxist journalists, many Third World diplomats, and theorists like Johan Galtung, who provide the analytic framework within which the structuralists' normative claims are justified. Structuralists believe that the source of global informational imbalance can be found in the West's desire to retain hegemony over formerly colonized areas. According to Herbert Schiller, a noted structural theorist, communication dominance has replaced more direct forms of political and military control. Control of communication and information is also said to be the means by which Western MNCs promote their economic interests at the expense of the developing nations (Schiller, 1976: 2–9).

Perhaps the foremost theorist of the structural school is Johan Galtung. Galtung's structural theory of imperialism seeks to demonstrate a connection between communication imperialism and cultural imperialism. For Galtung, the former necessarily leads to the latter. Galtung divides the world into two types of nations, the Center (developed) and the Periphery (underdeveloped). According to this schema, nations at the Center (i.e., the Western powers) dominate a "feudal network of communication." The Center owns the major news agencies, and "Center news takes up a much larger proportion of Periphery news media than vice versa" (Galtung, 1979: 165–166). As the imbalance perpetuates itself, ruling elites in the Periphery (e.g., the Third World) become more concerned with news from the Center than with news from other Periphery nations. The Center provides the definition of what is newsworthy for the Periphery. Journalists and media users in the Periphery, therefore, come to "see events with Center eyes." These factors in turn erode the cultural identity, national sovereignty, and political independence of developing states (see Chapter Four).

In light of these conditions, structuralists view the current order in international communication as extremely unjust and beyond redemption. The status quo is intolerable and cannot be saved through reforms. Reformists' offers of increased aid, technology, and training from the West to the Third World are derided as "benevolent cosmetic surgery" (Harris, 1981b: 360). Structuralists believe that the NWIO, like the NIEO, can be established only by razing the current international system and then building up a totally new order to replace it. Like the reformists, the structuralists also champion a free and balanced flow. Structuralists, however, place a much heavier emphasis on balance than on freedom.

The policy adjustments proposed by reformists on the MacBride Commission are given qualified support by the structuralists. However, the latter favor such reforms only if they are recognized as initial and partial steps toward more fundamental changes. Indeed, the same programs that Michael Anderson (a reformist) points to as progressive steps in international communication (e.g., training centers for Third World journalists) are condemned by Schiller as tools of economic neoimperialism (1976: 11).

Structuralists would push such reforms to their limits. They champion a "decolonized" and "democratized" media (see the treatment of critical theory in Chapter Two). Furthermore, many structuralists would go so far as to require the licensing of journalists, something the reformists (not to mention the conservatives) are very wary of. Licensing could serve as the first step toward international regulation and control of foreign correspondents.

In keeping with their criticisms of Western dominance, direct grants of communication technologies from the West also receive only qualified support by structural theorists. While Schiller does not rule out foreign technologies altogether, he does argue that LDCs must eventually become technologically self-sufficient (1976: 61). He fears the environmental dangers and domineering nature of Western high-tech industries. LDCs can be assured that communication systems will serve their particular social needs only when they come to rely on domestically produced hardwares. Only then will the research and development of technologies be geared to the unique requirements of Third World nations. Technological self-sufficiency also serves as an initial step toward political and economic autonomy by promoting the creation of "alternative [non-Western] social forms" (1976: 83).

A NEED FOR NEW RESEARCH

There is currently a dearth of empirical data on the international flow of information, and a lack of studies on the impact of global information flows on the political economies of developing nations. The MacBride Commission itself generated no new data. Therefore, a concomitant (perhaps even a prerequisite) to the study of policy options for nations and international organizations must be a careful study of the empirical relationships which currently exist in international information exchanges.

The claims made in the recent literature on these subjects are usually couched in only the most general of terms. After an imbalance of information flow is asserted to exist, one of two rhetorical moves is commonly made. The conservatives will point to alleged benefits derived from an imbalance in information traffic. The reformists and structuralists will stress what they see as the pernicious effects from the same condition of imbalance. The lack of empirical evidence which would clearly support either the position that the imbalance is beneficial, or the position that the imbalance produces demonstrable harm, leaves both sides arguing at cross-purposes.

The bulk of this study will test empirically key arguments made by the reformists and structuralists. Prior attempts to test Daniel Lerner's theory, a theory which serves as the basis for most of the conservative school's arguments, are also summarized at the conclusion of the next chapter. The focus will be on three points of contention: news flows, cultural imperialism, and the link between mass media and violence (see below). The particular arguments to be tested will be outlined in greater detail, and a manner in which each can be operationalized will be proposed. Results from the empirical studies will be analyzed with particular attention paid to the validity of the arguments with which the tests began. This manner of investigation will pull together so-called "normative" and "empirical" matters, and then bring both to bear on policy considerations. In so doing, the best available empirical evidence will reveal specific implications for national and international policy. A major deficiency in much contemporary political science is that it tries to keep empirical, normative, and policy concerns independent of one another. After these areas are created analytically, they too often become hypostatized as existing independently in the real world, where they are in fact so closely related as to be nearly inseparable. Perhaps this is one reason that political science often seems to have little direct relevance to current political issues and international problems.

TOPICS FOR NEW RESEARCH

Theories of Communication and Development

Chapter Two will address differing conceptions of news, theories of journalistic practice, and prior research into the relationship between communication and development in the Third World. It begins with a discussion of the two prevailing (and conflicting) definitions for the term "news." Each definition will be linked to its historical context and to particular journalistic practices. Finally, these two definitions of news—news as a saleable commodity versus news as a communal resource—will be tied to two schools of research into communication and modernization. This historical and theoretical discussion will then serve as background for the subsequent chapters that test certain arguments drawn from one of these schools of research—the structural school.

The International Flow of News

The imbalance of information flows is said to be forced upon developing nations due to a near-monopoly in media technology and wire service ownership enjoyed by the West. Developing nations charge that this monopoly creates biased and pro-Western accounts of news which are then foisted upon the Third World. Events in the West (on this account) come to the Third World almost exclusively through the Western TNNAs. What is even more pernicious and insulting in the view of some developing nations is the fact that Third World news, perhaps even news of events in their own countries, must also come largely from the Western TNNAs.

Although this is one of the most common arguments found in that literature which is critical of the current international information system, it is rarely worked out in any detail. The imbalance in news flow and the dependency of the Third World on Western news sources are assumed a priori with little hard evidence adduced to support these assumptions. Chapter Three delineates the flow of news by analyzing international reports carried within several of the most widely distributed and most influential Third World papers.

A more sophisticated extension of this method will also be used to test one aspect of Galtung's theory of structural imperialism. According to the Galtung thesis, news of other Third World countries would come to any particular developing nation through the wire service of its former colonial master. If foreign reports come to the media in former British colonies by way of Reuters (the British news service), then Galtung's thesis would be supported in that case. This would tend to verify Galtung's theory that contacts between the Periphery are dependent upon the intermediation of the Center. The news flow study will be used to discover if such a framework does indeed hold for North-South interactions.

International Communication and Cultural Imperialism

A central argument of the structuralists is that the Western monopoly on international information flows is a thinly veiled form of cultural imperialism. In Galtung's terms, Periphery nations have their news dominated by their respective Center nations. Instructors and curriculum for higher education are brought into the Periphery from the Center as well. Tourism in the Third World is said to be a function of similar cultural dependencies (Mowlana, 1986: 129). These conditions allegedly serve to increase the Periphery's desires and abilities to develop, think, and govern itself more and more like the Center. It is this process of westernizing the cultures of developing nations which is condemned by the phrase "cultural imperialism."

If cultural imperialism is caused in this way, one would expect developing nations that are highly dependent upon Western media to also be those LDCs which have gone the furthest in adopting a Western culture. Furthermore, nations that restrict the inflow of information from Western sources should be better able to resist the homogenization of their cultures to the Western model. These arguments will be subjected to a series of empirical tests in Chapter Four.

International Communication and Domestic Violence in the Third World

Critics of the current international order contend that Western news and information sources cause internal divisions and factional conflict within developing nations. The extreme case would be one in which broadcasting across national borders was used to incite ethnic hatred and racial violence. International agreements are in effect that try to curb or eliminate the dissemination of this sort of material (see McPhail, 1987: 301–304). Many developing nations, particularly those in sub-Saharan Africa, want an international system which could also control subtler forms of news and information that contribute to interethnic violence.

Generally stated, the claim is that inputs of Western news and information create increased domestic struggle for developing nations. Factors such as the demonstration effect are transmitted through Western programming and advertising. These conditions make ethnic groups within a developing nation less likely to cooperate and compromise. Each group comes to demand more and more of the limited national resources in order to attain a Western style of living. As tensions and conflicts increase between ethnic groups in a politics which is often a zero-sum game, subnational identities are reinforced. Thus efforts to overcome ethnic cleavages and attempts to build nationalism (e.g., a national identity) are severely compromised. Critics argue that developing nations must increase their control over foreign information in order to decrease national instability.

There is a wide range of national policies in the Third World in regard to the control of foreign news and information. Therefore, the opportunity exists to test whether those nations that restrict Western inputs do indeed experience a proportional increase in national stability. Such tests are the subject of Chapter Five.

Conclusions and Policy Implications

The final chapter will summarize the results gathered from the various empirical studies, keeping in mind the positions within structural theory that served as a starting point. The new data and the relationships newly identified will be assessed as a way of confirming or denying structural claims. Chapter Six will also consider some of the likely responses from the structuralists pertaining to the scope and methods of this study.

ANTICIPATED RESULTS

This examination of issues revolving around an NWIO builds consciously upon several arguments found in the existing literature. I identify the central theses put forth in the literature, articulate them in more detail, and bring the best available evidence to bear on them to see if it tends to support or refute these claims. I am concentrating specifically on three arguments, one of which is descriptive, and two others that propound causal relationships.

The descriptive project is presented in the news flow study of the third chapter and entails a more complete delineation of the current international information system. It answers such questions as: Where do the media in developing nations get most of their news? Does developmental journalism derive from different sources than spot (crisis) news? To what extent does the current system resemble the one that Galtung's structural theory of imperialism describes?

The analyses of causal relationships (to be found in the fourth and fifth chapters) will specify the effects which contemporary international information flows have upon the political economies of developing nations. Do mass media promote or hinder attempts to create a strong sense of nationalism in those states? Does it contribute to internal political instability? Is the current system one which forces developing nations to model themselves after the West, thus promoting cultural homogeneity?

If the data tend to support theories of structural imperialism, media and violence, and cultural homogenization, then developing nations will have a resource which is as yet denied them. They will have hard data to back their claims in reference to the necessity of a new information order. If the data are to the contrary, conservatives in the West will be able to defend their own claims on grounds other than ideological (e.g., the primacy of free speech). Arguments favoring a free flow would be given the substance they now lack. These facts, in turn, would cast doubts upon the necessity or wisdom of structural policies.

One strength of this study is its immediate relevance to policy considerations. Developing nations will be presented with a clearer picture of the political and economic impact of global information flows. This research should also assist nations that are members of the Organization for Economic Cooperation and Development (OECD) in addressing their policy voids concerning international communication. A better understanding of conditions in LDCs in regard to information and news is urgently needed to ensure a workable international climate between those nations and the West. The primary danger currently is that the dialogue on these and related issues will be broken off entirely due to the extreme ideological differences between the parties to the debate, and due to the lack of reliable data that either side can rely upon to support their position. The United States has started the West moving in the direction of cloture by its departure from Unesco. Nonaligned states such as Zimbabwe seem only too happy to follow suit by denying access to the Western media.[1]

The scope of this work is admittedly restricted in some respects, as no attempt is made to construct a grand theory of political communication.

However, this restriction can also be viewed as one of the inherent strengths of the overall project. While the research is not conducted at the highest levels of theorizing, it is closely and necessarily related to difficult political problems and real-world policy alternatives. Therein lies its primary importance and its immediate utility.

NOTE

1. Zimbabwe is a good example of a Third World nation going to ideological extremes, making foreign journalists persona non grata when they are deemed by the Mugabe regime to have filed biased or anti-governmental reports. As one leader of the Third World's campaign for an NWIO, and as host of the 1987 Cominac II conference on global communication for nonaligned nations, Zimbabwe's approach to these issues is almost certain to gain additional supporters if the West (and especially the United States) continues its current policy of ignoring calls for less stringent reforms.

2

Two Conceptions of "News"

Issues of international news reporting have become increasingly politicized throughout recent years. The campaign for a New World Information Order (NWIO) has moved the debate over international systems of communication to center stage in many international organizations. Some nonaligned nations, such as Kenya and Zimbabwe, have charged that Western correspondents are overtly biased in their coverage, and have therefore closed their borders to selected reporters.[1] Groups of nonaligned states, such as the members of ASEAN (the Association of Southeast Asian Nations), have agreed that a ban on particular Western correspondents in one nation will mean a ban in all (Righter, 1978: 214). Because OECD nations enjoy vast advantages in informational resources, nonaligned nations now tend to politicize international debates while adopting obstructionist stances (see Chapter One). Taken together, these and other closely related traumas in the international body politic amount to a current "crisis in international news" (Richstad and Anderson, 1981).

The crisis in international news has many sources. Debates over an NWIO have addressed a plethora of complicated issues. Yet there is consistently one central point of contention: what is "news"? Much of the scholarly and diplomatic debate about an NWIO revolves around this seemingly simple question. Proponents and opponents of the NWIO start with two distinctly different definitions of what "news" is and what it should stand for in an international context. As a result, the two sides take different positions on what sort of "news values" journalists should uphold, and on the proper political role for mass media at the national and international levels. A thorough discussion of these two conceptions of news—news as a commodity and news as a social resource—will reveal the historical development, economic basis, and political implications of each definition.

NEWS IN THE WEST OR NEWS AS A COMMODITY

The most concise description of news in a Western context is that news here is treated as a commodity. Western media provide international news in the form of "a merchandise rather than a service" and news stories "are selected for their impact, exoticism, ability to entertain" (Righter, 1978:41). News items are collected in bits and distributed in markets according to their utility and consumer tastes. The history of international news reporting shows that news has taken this particular form largely due to market forces in advanced capitalist industrial societies. Furthermore, the contents of international news have also been largely determined by these same market imperatives. News as a commodity was developed in the late nineteenth century, primarily in Great Britain and the United States, and was firmly established by the year 1900.[2] Historically, it is a conception of news that has served particular economic interests and catered to specific cultural tastes.

If asked to define "news," most Westerners would probably reply that it is factual, up-to-the-minute information regarding recent occurrences. A news report tells what has happened as well as when, where, why, and how. A well-written news story on international affairs should also be brief, to the point, and clear about how the foreign event relates to the reader's own life. Not all cultures agree that this constitutes "good" news reporting, but these are all characteristics of news as a commodity.

The earliest uses of "news" referred to something novel or previously unencountered. After 1500, common usage employed "news" much as it is used today: to refer to "new occurrences as a subject of report or talk" (*Oxford English Dictionary*, vol. VII, 1970: 119). Systematic international news gathering did not arise until late in the eighteenth century when newspaper editors began collecting foreign newspapers and then reprinted their local reports as foreign news (Desmond, 1980: 37). At this time, however, foreign reporting was nominal and foreign correspondents did not yet exist. International news did not approach anything like its current scope or volume, nor did the first international news agencies appear, until the age of high imperialism, the middle and late nineteenth century.

Capitalism, as Anthony Smith argues, has always been an "information system" as well as a system of finance and production (1980: 73). The development of international capitalism incorporated more and more of the world's unexploited areas into the global market. Corporations, transportation, and stock markets became "inextricably combined" into an integrated system. "At the heart of it there has to be information, for the central concept of capitalism is the market and, in a global system... markets [depend on] prices and values [which] are assessed through the distribution of regular reliable information" (p. 74). With the expansion of Western colonialism came the creation of a global communication network based on the technology of undersea telegraph cables (perfected in the middle of the nineteenth century). In Smith's terms, the worldwide information network quickly became "a fundamental support" for the development of international capitalism.

London became the news center of the world because it was already the center of international trade, finance, and commodity pricing (Desmond, 1980: 62). Of course, gathering news from around the world required substantial financial resources. Support for the early international press came almost entirely from industrialists, bankers, and financiers who sought to promote their own success. Because no single newspaper could afford the cost of telegraph cables, foreign correspondents, and independent stringers around the globe, independent news agencies which could defray these costs through client subscriptions became necessary. The first international telegraph lines that made news agencies financially necessary also provided the hardware and saleable goods to make them economically viable (Desmond, 1980: 132).

By 1855, three international news agencies existed: Wolff in Germany, Havas (precursor to the Agence France Presse [AFP]) in France, and Reuters in London. Of these, only Reuters remains; and it is Reuters which has had by far the greatest impact on the development of international news reporting as we know it today.

Julius Reuter established his first news agency in Aachen, France, in 1849, but only two years later moved his operations to London. Originally, Reuter supplied commercial news to bankers, investors, and merchants, while Havas and Wolff carried other sorts of news as well. Reuter was shrewd enough to put his offices in the London financial district and quickly concluded a deal with the London Stock Exchange to provide stock market quotations from the financial centers on the continent. In return, Reuter received privileged access to information from the London Exchange. Reuter's first customers were exclusively bankers, stock brokers, traders, merchants, and business firms (Desmond, 1980: 146).

In order to increase his clientele, however, Reuter realized that he had to carry noncommercial news as well. To attract small newspapers to his service, Reuter established a Special Service in 1890 to carry sensational journalism. Since 1880, sensationalism had been rising in popularity among newspaper editors in the United States and in England as a means to create a greater appeal among the growing urban masses. To attract a wider readership, "they departed from patterns of substantial news and information and from considerations of accuracy and truth to present stories of crimes and scandals, disasters and accidents of special violence, riots and disturbances ... the more sensational the better" (Desmond, 1980: 333). Reuter created his Special Service in response to competition from the sensationalist Dalziel agency which was owned by the London *Times* (the *Times* refused Reuter's service and competed vigorously with it). In the early years of international news reporting, competition was vicious. Those agencies which did not follow popular trends such as that of sensationalism soon went out of business. Even after the Reuters agency later dropped the Special Service, it was obliged to integrate some of the sensationalist style into its regular service (Desmond, 1980: 345).

Within twenty years of opening his London agency, Reuter came to dominate international news gathering. In most cases, Reuters took the lead, setting the tone and form of foreign reporting. Other international agencies were forced to adopt most of Reuters' techniques and tried to establish themselves in regions not monopolized by Reuters (e.g., central Europe and Latin America). Following Reuters' example, agencies supplied two broad types of foreign news to two types of customers. Trading communities were supplied with "instant, exact and copious commerical and political information" which had direct importance for their overseas holdings. The other market consisted of "a large number of smaller newspapers whose readers wanted romantic headlines, big stories and not too much substance" (Smith, 1980: 77).

In 1857, Reuter signed an exclusive contract to supply foreign news to the United States through the New York Associated Press (NYAP, which, after several reorganizations, became the Associated Press in 1900). In turn, NYAP supplied the foreign news published in over a score of major American cities in the East and Mideast. Accordingly, the conventions and substance of Reuters international reports came to be accepted in the United States as the standard for interstate news. There was, however, one important element of journalistic style which originated largely in the United States, later to be carried across the Atlantic through the agreement between Reuters and NYAP. This was the notion that "objectivity" is essential to news writing.

This element of impartiality, like other characteristics of news as a commodity, developed in the mid- to late-nineteenth century, and also received its impetus from the dictates of the marketplace. Before the American Civil War, news reporting was characterized by "florid description" and "subjective comment." Correspondents often mixed their own views, judgments, and personal feelings with the facts of the report. This highly stylized form of journalism was popular, but with the advent of telegraphs and the demands for quick reports on the war, it became too costly. In order to shorten the story (to save on telegraph costs, which were charged by the word), a new style of news writing was developed for war correspondents. This was the summary lead/body style which is so familiar today.

In the story's lead, journalists were instructed to state the "five Ws" (who, what, when, where, why). Then in the body, each of these aspects of the story could be elaborated. Opinions, judgments, and personal reactions to the war were to be confined to the last few paragraphs. If the story ran too long, editors could start at the bottom and cut out paragraphs as they moved up toward the lead. Editors came to prefer the lead/body format because it seemed to produce more economy and clarity in news stories. This style, begun in the United States in the 1860s, came to "set a pattern for the press of other countries" (Desmond, 1980: 217). Thus it became the one major American contribution to news as a commodity. Just as other elements of news form and content were disseminated in this nation due to contracts between news agencies, so this style was disseminated through the NYAP, via Reuters, to the rest of the world.

By 1900, news on international affairs was presented in a particular format, and it dealt with particular substantive matters. It was primarily news of either a commercial or a sensational nature. It was preferred in the summary lead/body format. The five Ws were to be stated at the outset of each story and all subjective comment was relegated to the story's conclusion (if not cut out altogether). News of the day, especially international news, possessed all three of the fundamental characteristics which Marx attributed to commodities. It developed within the historical context of industrialized, capitalist society. It contained a use value (e.g., information for economic gain, or to cater to an interest in sensationalism). Finally, it was a result of human labor, produced for the use of others, and exchanged within a capitalist market system (Marx: 1–7).

Such was the nature of international news at the turn of the century. By 1910, the "Big Four" of contemporary international news (AFP, Associated Press [AP], Reuters, and United Press International [UPI]) existed either in their current form or as the immediate predecessor to their current form (Havas became AFP after World War II and the United Press Association [UPA], established in 1907, became UPI in 1958). Including the Wolff agency, there were five international news agencies in the early twentieth century; two American, one British, one French, and one German. Each of these agencies, due to customer demand, felt compelled to write their stories from a national perspective. American agencies wrote foreign reports with a tie to American interests, and so forth. Added to the stylistic requirements of the lead/body format was a new sensitivity to local values back home. Foreign assignments were to be "treated like a local assignment. The diversity [being] so great... making order of it for the reader almost require[d] that it be explained in the relatively 'local' framework of a set of cultural and intellectual perceptions" (Righter, 1978: 59). According to Righter, national slant is still exhibited in Western reporting today, "however many foreign journalists an agency hires, and however much material may even be a rewrite of the national press or news agency output of the host country."

One recent study of the style handbooks utilized by major news organizations shows that journalists are systematically trained to employ this fashion of news writing. These handbooks stress that "to be simple and precise is at the same time to identify facts that are significant to an individual's social life." Alexander quotes from a typical style book, which admonishes its users to remember that "[e]very word must be understood by the ordinary man, every sentence must be clear at a glance, and every story must say something about people. There must never be a doubt about its relevance to our daily life" (Alexander, 1981: 41).

Not only did the major agencies separate their reports according to national perspective, but they also divided their world beats along the lines of colonial boundaries and imperial interests. As early as 1870, the so-called Ring Combination (Havas, Reuters, and Wolff) had divided the world into regions with each member of the cartel having exclusive rights to collect and sell interstate news in particular areas. Reuters had the rights to all of the British Empire, Egypt and the Middle East, and most of Asia. The French agency (Havas) was given rights to the French Empire as well as Latin American news (largely by default). The German agency was confined primarily to central Europe. With the advent of the American agencies, cartel members found themselves competing for news sources and clients in the areas of American hegemony (e.g., Latin American and the southern Pacific). This competition was set aside briefly as agreements brought AP and UPA into the cartel, but a resurgence of rivalries brought about the Ring's demise in 1934 (Smith, 1980: 81–82).

It was during the era of the international news cartel that most of the structural arrangements in interstate communication were established, structures which critics argue persist to this day. The paths of news flow went from the colonial periphery to the industrialized center, with little or no "horizontal" communication among non-Western regions. Reuters was the most vigorous in establishing the first technological links, and in gaining control of the hardware necessary to news flows. Reuters dominated the Ring Combination due to the fact that the British Empire had a virtual monopoly over undersea telegraph cables (Desmond, 1980: 163). Because Britannia ruled the waves, Reuters was able to rule the news hardware under the waves. Reuters sank its first privately owned cable in 1866; and by 1880, additional cables enabled it to open bureaus in Australia, China, India, and Japan.

Control of, or privileged access to, the hardware necessary for international news flow has always provided a great advantage to any agency able to acquire it. The drive to maximize profits and increase efficiency has created a long-term trend in the international news business toward increasing concentration and monopolization. Today there are four giants of international news and each is a multinational corporation (MNC): AFP, AP, Reuters, and UPI. As these transnational news agencies (TNNAs), move into regions around the world, they bring more than just reporters armed with pad and pencil. They also import a whole series of complex communication technologies over which they retain control and from which substantial problems develop for the political economies of developing nations. A postwar campaign by American TNNAs to break the British stranglehold on control of these technologies produced the first arguments favoring a "free flow" of news and information between nations (Schiller, 1976: 26–29; Smith, 1980: 44). This brings us to a final aspect of news as a commodity: the relationship between modes of news reporting and political ideologies.

News as a Commodity and Political Ideologies

Numerous studies by sociologists and communication theorists have tried to establish whether mass media work to maintain the status quo, or promote social and political change. Results from these studies run the gamut from claiming that media (news media in particular) are conservative political forces, to claiming that they are the means for radical change. However, there is strong agreement from both camps that "news suggests a general outlook on the world, an ideology, a frame of interpretation" (Katz and Szecsko, 1981: 7).

Following the lead of Reuters, international news agencies historically have catered to the needs and tastes of two consumer groups. Political and economic elites are provided with news that affects their vested interests. The general public is provided with news that satisfies desires for the unusual and sensational. Golding has argued that the "historical process" which led to "the development of news as a service to elite groups" has created a situation in which "the basic goals and values which surround journalism refer to the needs and interests" of elites (1981: 79). Because news media need a broader audience than just elites to stay in business, Golding goes on to point out that reporting must draw on common social values and assumptions in order to reach a mass audience. The history of news agency clientele supports Golding's thesis. This is not, however, an argument which crudely asserts that the news media are nothing more than a tool for elite domination. Golding is at pains to point this out:

Analyses which see news as necessarily a product of powerful groups in society, designed to provide a view of the world consonant with the interests of these groups, simplify the situation too far to be helpful. The occupational routines and beliefs of journalists do not allow a simple conduit between the ruling ideas of the powerful and their distribution via the airwaves. (p. 80)

The important point is that these "occupational routines" (elaborated below) preclude the development of views which might question the legitimacy of elite interest and/or the prevailing consensus.

Recall that the summary lead/body format was originally designed to remove such subjective elements as ideology from news stories. However, another recent study has shown that the criteria of good lead writing depend not only on the five Ws, but also on how well the lead makes a strong normative and moral point (Alexander, 1981). "The lead is a device for summing up the 'significance' of the data-event by relating it, implicitly, to what people would have expected to happen in similar situations or to more general value judgments that would normally be applicable" (p. 20). A style that was originally meant to remove normative and ideological aspects from news stories seems to have become the primary vehicle for retaining these features.

Studies of the organizational structure of large news agencies have revealed an additional source of ideological bias. While many journalists would like to believe that the news is just "out there" waiting to be actively pursued, Golding has revealed how the standard operating procedures (SOPs) of news agencies produce reports which are largely "passive, routine, limited, selective." The selection of events to cover is far from random or merely contingent on the course of world affairs. SOP for any news agency is to reduce uncertainty by "plotting events in advance and determining which are to become news" (p. 70). The use of the standard news diary (a listing of routine news items) predetermines to a large extent what is defined as "news." Heavy reliance even by the TNNAs on "a few defined institutional sources, most notably government," also means that the contents of the news are highly "bureaucratized" and "routinized" (see below) according to institutional norms. These practices are the "working rules" of news media which come to be defended as "news values" by strident opponents of the NWIO such as Leonard Sussman (1981). These working rules, or SOPs, are derived from the two classic determinants of story gathering: "perceptions of the audience" and "availability of material." Therefore, news is not pursued wherever necessary and regardless of its interest. Furthermore, Golding argues, it is only because these SOPs are employed over time that they become "imbued with the lustre of good practice." This is a "classic case of making a virtue of necessity" (p. 77). What were originally commercial necessities become "ethical imperatives" (Schiller, 1976: 29). Because the SOPs produce only a partial view of the world (due to preselection and predetermination of the newsworthy), and because news media exist first and foremost to provide service to elites, SOPs invariably produce an ideology (partial view) largely consistent with that of the national elite's (Golding, 1981: 79-81).

Mass media audiences also receive a partial (even partisan) view of the world due to the bureaucratized nature of news gathering and reporting. A bureaucratized media is one in which legitimized institutions are primarily responsible for defining the content of news reports. It is also a form of media organization that facilitates governmental management of the news. News media rely heavily upon information that is centralized by bureaucracies and facts that are generated by bureaucracies. Rather than pursuing facts objectively and impartially wherever they are available, news is gathered primarily through "[b]ureaucratized and routinized interactions between and among workers in legitimated institutions" (Tuchman, 1981: 88).

Studies of bureaucratized media (Altheide and Johnson, 1980; Bennett, 1983; Tuchman, 1981) reveal that in order to meet deadlines (and according to SOPs) news organizations from the small-town newspaper, to the national networks, to the TNNAs rely upon institutions to tell them things as varied as the amount of financial losses from a fire; the extent of government's stability and popularity; estimates of anti-governmental support, as well as their aims and methods; the impact of inflation (in dollar rather than human terms); the noise levels produced by a supersonic transport (from the Federal Aviation Administation rather than from the people living in the flight path). These "facts" are assumed to be "essentially correct and disinterested." Facts from other sources, therefore, are "soft" and "non-objective." This "reliance on centralized sources may blind reporters to occurrences" or to alternate interpretations of a given occurrence. Because the TNNAs themselves are large bureaucracies, they can use their institutional weight to gain privileged access to governmental sources (Desmond, 1980: 312), which inevitably increases their reliance on these official sources. Finally, we find that pre-bureaucratized groups or groups not legitimated by the extant political order (e.g., guerrilla and anti-governmental organizations in Central America) are largely frozen out, given no access to the most important news outlets. The official line then becomes the only voice which is heard. Bennett (1983: 55) and Tuchman (1981: 89) point out that marginal groups are then forced to seek media coverage through the creation of radical or violent events.

Media news coverage presents a partial view of the world and upholds the prevalent political ideology by catering to the interests and needs of certain groups; through the format of lead writing and administrative SOP; and due to its bureaucratic nature. But one can also say a great deal more about specific political purposes for which news as a commodity has been employed. In its earliest forms, international news was full of "imperial imagery" and was used to rally support for colonial wars and imperial conquests (Smith, 1980: 77). In the early twentieth century, the major international agencies became even more closely dependent upon, and associated with, their national governments. Reuters' managing director was even made head of British war propaganda in World War I—taking much of the agency's material directly from the War Cabinet—while he remained as head of the agency (*ibid.*: 80).

The implications of news as a commodity must also be drawn out for the international political context. Early postwar theories of development by Lerner, de Sola Pool, Pye, and others held that urbanization and increased literacy would produce modernization in the Third World. Increased literacy would stimulate media use and create a more productive workforce. A free press and enhanced economic output would then produce democratic politics and modern development in those nations. We now know that these theories were overly optimistic. Indeed, reliance upon Western styles of news and imported technology may have brought increased cultural and economic dependence to many less developed countries (LDCs), rather than providing them with more independence and autonomy. Disillusionment with Western-style development has made the LDCs skeptical of the informational theories on which many were based.

As Western economic models were introduced and Western TNNAs expanded their operations in the LDCs, those nations became increasingly reliant on foreign technologies and MNCs. TNNAs themselves are dependent on the current international arrangements which safeguard the interest of multinationals (e.g., protections against nationalization and the right of compensation). As multinationals, the TNNAs are economically dependent on these safeguards and on their ability to transfer costs and revenues across national borders. A standard TNNA response to charges that they exploit LDCs is that bureaus in developing nations consistently operate at a loss; therefore, they could not stay in business without economic protections. Support for news as a commodity and for the agencies which provide it must necessarily be support for an international status quo that protects multinationals, allowing them a free hand to pursue their interests in LDCs as they see fit.

A demand for a free reign to Western MNCs is consistent with the insistence by NWIO opponents for a free flow of international news. This position transposes to the international arena arguments favoring free speech which were originally developed by liberal theorists for a national setting. Although this move raises all sorts of theoretical problems regarding "levels of analysis" and the suitability of political arguments created in a national context to international relations, to deal with these issues here would take us too far afield. Clearly, there can be no doubt that most arguments in favor of a free flow are based on political values held near and dear to liberalism.

One reason that liberal arguments seem to shift so effortlessly from a national to an international setting is that the moral basis of current international relations is essentially "the international analogue of nineteenth-century liberalism" (Beitz, 1979: 66). Beitz has shown quite convincingly that the fundamental values of the nation-state system—national sovereignty, and nonintervention into the internal affairs of another state—are the international equivalents of certain classic liberal values for individuals—that each person is an autonomous source of ends, and each individual is morally free to arrange his or her own personal affairs (self-regarding actions). Of course, even in liberal society (and certainly in international relations) such values are often violated in practice. But the fact remains that a commitment to the current international status quo is also a commitment to certain liberal values (and this by no means excludes the socialist nations).

To summarize, the general implications of news as a commodity for international relations are as follows. To promote or protect news in the Western form of a commodity requires that one defend certain characteristically liberal values as well as certain features of the international economic status quo. News as a commodity requires the protection of MNCs and the defense of liberal values which are the moral basis of the nation-state system. It should also be clear by now why those nations which have been disillusioned by the failures of liberal development theory, those which desire international reforms to curb the power of multinationals, and those which have deep reservations about certain liberal values would also be suspicious of diplomats and journalists who defend news as a commodity. These are the nations that are campaigning for the NWIO, and these are the nations which believe that the political commitments underlying news values of Western journalism are contrary to the best interests of the LDCs. This brings us to the second conception of news, a notion offered by the proponents of the NWIO: news as a social good.

NEWS IN THE DEVELOPING NATIONS OR NEWS AS A SOCIAL GOOD

In contrast to news as a commodity—a concept that developed in the age of nineteenth-century colonialism—news as a social good developed during the twentieth-century campaign for decolonization. This was (and is) a time during which former colonies tried to modernize quickly through promoting rapid development. LDCs tried to broaden and improve their industries, educational institutions, and the general social welfare all at the same time—and each as quickly as possible. During this period of so-called "late-late" development, others have tried to accomplish in a few short decades that which took Western nations centuries to establish. Such an undertaking required large-scale projects of social engineering and more centralized planning.

Under these conditions, developing nations began to consider the news media and its products as social goods. All national assets (including information) came to be seen as resources held in common, and under absolute sovereign control of the state. Oil reserves and news items were viewed as essentially equivalent in this important respect. Information was to be employed as a tool for rapid development, just as other national resources such as labor and mineral deposits. In fact, news and information regarding all national assets was itself a resource which allowed these other goods and services to be more efficiently utilized.

Many Third World leaders now take the position that communication must be controlled and directed by the state. News should concentrate on reports regarding nationwide projects. Such reports are at the heart of the style of developmental journalism. Developmental journalism centers on long-range works of modernization and its reports are directed at informing the population. It displays a particular concern for reaching the poorest and most underdeveloped areas. In this respect, developmental journalism serves as a substitute means for educating the public (due to lack of schools) about the current national and global situation.

When reporting on international events, journalists of the developmental school go to greater lengths than their Western counterparts in including both the historical background and the possible long-range implications of the isolated data-event. Again this is an educative as well as a purely informative approach. In Western societies, these other aspects of a story are usually gotten from non-media sources (such as educational institutions) or are confined to the "op-ed" page. Due to a lack of alternate means, developmental journalists seek to educate as they inform their readers.

In a national context, developmental journalism is exemplified by the *Famille et Development* project of Francophone Africa. This service covers many nations and provides information on health and family planning while "rigorously eschewing all other political messages" (Smith, 1980: 149). These are undertakings that attempt to bring communities with low literacy rates into the public discussion regarding development while, at the same time, providing them with useful information and promoting self-education. This is *not* journalism that merely serves as political propaganda to indoctrinate the public to the official government line, contrary to claims by Righter (1978: 18) and others.

Due to a lack of financial resources, a decentralized media structure is not currently possible in most LDCs. In most cases, it is only the central government that has the funds necessary to keep a news agency operating. Therefore, news agencies in the Third World must be either heavily subsidized or state-owned. News coming into the nation is usually "filtered" through the government before it reaches the newspapers or broadcast media, as the state itself is the subscriber to foreign wire services (Righter, 1981: 61). Surprisingly enough, this does not prevent the media in many LDCs from adopting standards of critical journalism, despite such governmental controls (Smith, 1980: 150). News going out of these nations, especially that which goes to the developmental news services such as the Inter-Press Service and the Nonaligned News Pool, usually comes directly from the national ministry of information.

The technology and expertise needed to operate Third World news agencies come almost exclusively from the Western TNNAs and telecommunication industries. Furthermore, as another legacy of the colonial era, the majority of LDC agencies were originally established by the French and British, modeled on their own news media (Katz and Wedell, 1977). These conditions have contributed to the economic dependence of the South on the North, and imported technologies have created problems for attempts at internal modernization.

The Ideology of News as a Social Good

The political ideology that supports news as a commodity is subtly concealed but is there nonetheless. The political ideology of news as a social good, on the other hand, is consciously overt. It is an anti-imperialist ideology, and a product of the campaign by developing nations against what they see as a neocolonial international order. Political independence was achieved by these nations over the past twenty to thirty years, but they believe that their national sovereignty and autonomy remain severely compromised by arrangements in international economics and technology. According to Smith,

> It did not occur to many people until the last decade or so that information lay at the root of sovereignty and that the movement for independence would have to continue beyond the political stage into economic and informational struggles of equal intensity to those which had led to the first stages of the post-colonial era. (1980: 58)

LDCs now charge that it is necessary to break the structures and patterns of news flows which remain essentially neocolonial and "vertical" communication, with little "horizontal" communication taking place between the LDCs themselves. Third World leaders have also expressed their desires to employ national communication industries to increase national unity and to promote a shared sense of national identity (Katz and Wedell, 1977: 26–27). Most of these leaders currently think that Western-style news and information services contribute to social divisions (Smith, 1980: 156).

Perhaps the most central claim advanced by Third World critics in the midst of the NWIO debate is that current patterns of international news flows contribute to the displacement of traditional, indigenous cultures in LDCs by Western values and modes of thought (Galtung, 1979: 165–166; Masmoudi, 1981: 80–81; Schiller, 1976: 8–20). Anthony Smith quotes Juan Somavia,[3] head of the Latin American Institute for Transnational Studies (ILET), on this point, charging that the current international news system is "a vehicle for transmitting values and lifestyles to Third World countries which stimulates the type of consumption and the type of society necessary to the transnational expansion of capital" (1980: 101–102).

We have already seen how support for the Western free press and advocacy of news as a commodity are necessarily pro–status quo. To support news in the form of a social good (and those elements of the NWIO that address this matter), on the other hand, is to support many of the contemporary attempts at global reform. The NWIO serves as an integral part of a larger effort to restructure international relations. The NWIO is seen by its proponents as a necessary concomitant to the New International Economic Order (MacBride Commission, 1981: 46, 53). Those who advocate news as a social good, therefore, are necessarily reformists, oftentimes even revolutionaries, in the international context.

The aim of the NWIO on the conceptual level is to replace the Western notion of news as a commodity with that of news as a social good. In discussing Somovia's work for ILET, Righter quotes him as charging that news from TNNAs destroys "authentic cultural values" and subjugates Third World interests to those of the developed nations through "political penetration" of the former by the latter's news agencies. This is based on news as a commodity, news that "responds to the laws of the market," and news for which "the criteria used in selection are always contrary to the interests of sovereign independence." Somovia's "antidote" for these problems (according to Righter) is to replace news as a commodity with "information as a social good, in the service of development" (1978: 107–108).

Contrary to Righter's own claims, however, developmental journalism and its notion of news as a social good differs significantly from Leninist journalism, which merely repeats the official line and seeks to build support for the ruling elites. There are numerous examples of government-owned or -subsidized press institutions in the Third World (e.g., in India, Kenya, Tanzania) which seek to advance the style of developmental journalism while, at the same time, employing "the same faculty of critical examination, the same kind of investigative instinct as libertarian journalism" (Smith, 1980: 172; see also 148–150). In effect, this would require that we add a fifth category, that of developmental journalism, to the classic essay by Siebert (1956) on the "four theories of the press"—a new classification that does not fall neatly into any of the old categories. For too long, following Siebert's analysis, the Western view has been that any press not allowed the freedoms enjoyed in this part of the world must necessarily be a propagandistic press. This view represents a gross oversimplification. Under a commitment to developmental news standards, governmental control and critical evaluations of national policy are not mutually exclusive (see Table 2.1). Advocates of the developmental style would argue that critical standards are essential to their task. Such a skeptical posture facilitates evaluations of governmental performance—checking to see if gains achieved through policies of development live up to official promises (thus protecting the interests of the masses—see Aggarwala, 1979). Therefore, the choice is not merely one of either a free press or a Leninist media. There is also a middle road, the developmental press, that seeks to combine elements of the other two. This is the road that LDCs have mapped out for themselves.

On the other hand, it certainly is true that many supporters of the NWIO

Table 2.1:
A Comparison of Three Press Institutions

VARIABLE	UNSTANDARDIZED COEFFICIENT	STANDARDIZED COEFFICIENT	t-RATIO
MI	3321.0	.42	1.18
PF	128908.0	.69	2.05
GNP	-11.0	-.37	1.02

Dependent Variable = LUX   intercept = 155,406
R^2 = .48   adjusted R^2 = .17   N = 9   s.e. = 187,188

LUX = US dollars spent on selected imported luxury items
         (source: United Nations, 1982)
    other sources: see Tables 4.1 and 4.2

employ an anti-American rhetoric much like that of our Soviet critics. However, this fact is due more to the popularity in the Third World of neo-marxian economic analyses of the structuralist and *dependencia* schools than to a desire on the part of Third World journalists and editors to emulate TASS (the Soviet news service). The unpopularity of TASS in the Third World media is evident in their general reluctance to reprint its reports, even though they are provided free of charge (Smith, 1980: 70).

Like news as a commodity, news as a social good leaves much to be desired. The media practices based on either conception of news allow for several areas of improvement. One can study the deficiencies of each by contrasting both to a third model on which to base news media organizations. This is the model of the "democratized media."

CRITICAL THEORY AND DEMOCRATIZED MEDIA

The democratized media refers to those media reforms based on critical theories of communication. Critical communication theory is among the intellectual heirs to the Frankfurt school of political theory. Under Jurgen Habermas at the Max Planck Institut, the specific focus of many critical theorists has been that of social communication. This group is unified by its primary concern for the political nature of speech and other forms of communication. The phrase "democratized media" is one employed by proponents of the NWIO as well as by the critical theorists; however, these two groups use it to refer to different contexts. Mustapha Masmoudi (former Tunisian Minister of Information) has used the term to identify those parts of the NWIO aimed at international reform, primarily an increase in horizontal flows of information. The democratized media would promote more news and information exchanges between Third World nations. It would create "machinery for cooperation and mutual assistance between developing countries, such as [the] Press Agency Pool of the Nonaligned Countries" (1981: 91).

NWIO advocates and critical theorists share a common concern in media restructuring. Both groups would decentralize and demonopolize media firms. Again, Masmoudi's interest is in international restructuring: "ensuring equal and equitable use of all communication media, including satellites" (1981: 91). Critical theorists have directed their energies much more toward reforms of the national media in advanced industrial societies. They would break up the national monopolies of media capital owners. They would transfer media control from the private owners (e.g., networks) to media producers (e.g., artists, editors, reporters, writers). They also argue in favor of the "political activation of the masses for communicative emancipation" (Lanigan and Strobl, 1981: 146). This last point would mean bringing pre-bureaucratic, nonbureaucratic, and nonlegitimated social groups into the process of informational exchange.

An examination of the democratized media of the NWIO in practice must include a recognition of the fact that they are more bureaucratized than the Western media. Media practices of the NWIO may be a platform for international change, but they can also be used to impede political reforms within developing nations. Media in these nations can be subjected to heavier governmental controls than Western media, as news flowing in and out of the Third World is, in most cases, directly controlled by the central government. This is what Western opponents of the NWIO condemn the most. They argue that there is only one choice: between a free, open Western-style press and a tightly controlled Soviet-style government press (see Sussman, 1981). Such crude oversimplifications only obscure the real issues and contribute to the international climate of antagonism over news flows. Developmental journalism cannot be simply equated with Leninist journalism.

On the other hand, the Western free press, based on the notion of news as a commodity, is also badly in need of improvement. The democratized media of critical theory was developed to promote media reform in advanced industrialized states. The ideological content of Western news is obscured, and even denied to exist. The bulk of critical theory research in communication has been directed at debunking these claims (Lanigan and Strobl, 1981: 144). Western media is overreliant upon "official," "legitimate" institutions that define what the news is. This bureaucratized media can allow for governmental controls on the news that—while they are less visible—rival the effectiveness of more overt tactics used by nonaligned governments. Nonbureaucratic groups get little or no media coverage and therefore have no opportunity to express their positions. To get coverage, they turn to violence or civil disobedience. Even these more extreme tactics yield only nominal coverage, usually sensationalist reports (the best treatment to date of these issues is Bennett's [1983] discussion of what he calls the "normalized media").

Furthermore, foreign correspondents from the West are not sufficiently trained for international reporting. They carry little knowledge of the relevant historical background with them when they rush off to cover invasions in the Caribbean or elections in Buenos Aires. Fear that reporters will lose their "perspective" (ethnocentrism?) has created the SOP of rotating foreign correspondents from one capital city to another, rarely leaving them in one place for more than three years at a time (Desmond, 1980: 312). Even training foreign nationals to report for TNNAs leaves many of these problems unresolved (Smith, 1980: 72). Because the reports reaching the West are often short-sighted, incomplete, and disjointed, the West works in a "policy vacuum" or suffers from a "policy void" (Spero, 1982). This misinformation reaches the media consumers in the West (congressmen, party leaders, voters) and becomes the basis of faulty judgments on foreign policy.

Finally, as each conception of news has its own peculiar faults, and as each is linked to particular developmental policies in the Third World, misconceptions about the mass media necessarily lead to political and economic failures in LDCs. Two approaches to using media in service of development have characterized prior literature on the subject. Each school of thought on communication for development in the Third World also has its own preferred definition of the term "news" as well.

TWO THEORIES OF COMMUNICATION AND DEVELOPMENT

The question of how modern communication can best serve the needs of developing nations has sparked both a policy debate and a theoretical debate. The *policy* debate has revolved around the negotiations within the United Nations Educational, Scientific, and Cultural Organization (Unesco) on a new information order. This dialogue addresses such areas as developmental policies in the Third World; foreign policies of the West which affect the Third World; standards of international justice and equity; and topics in international law (e.g., the right to communicate). The *theoretical* debate is being fought out in academic circles and professional journals. It raises such issues as the following: What types of information best serve the ends of modernization in LDCs? What means of distributing such information in the Third World are the most efficient? Is the structure of international communication neocolonial? Many of the theoretical issues became politically salient due only to the nature of the NWIO policy debate. The remainder of this study will put the policy debates within the context of the following two theories of development.

The Lerner Thesis

Early postwar development theory—strongly influenced by Daniel Lerner's seminal work *The Passing of Traditional Society*—was based, in part, on certain propositions about how communication operates in a modern, industrialized society. Urban growth necessitates increased specialization, differentiation, and division of labor. Specialized expertise becomes necessary to operate modern industries, businesses, and schools. A modern or modernizing industrial nation also must rely on particular types of rationality (e.g., ends-means calculations) and particular forms of specialized information (see Frey, 1973: 377–379). According to Lerner's thesis, what is needed primarily are the "bare facts" and the latest, updated information that will allow for effective rational decisions. Raw data is provided to utilitarian decision-makers to enable them to make the best choice of means to ends.

There is also a unique mechanism that has proved (according to this thesis) to yield the best production of this raw data. That is the free market. Employing arguments not significantly different from those of J. S. Mill and Thomas Jefferson (see Wills, 1979: 316–317), Western theorists of development see a free market of news and ideas as the best aid to political and economic development in all nations (see also Merrill, 1981). The free flow of news and information serves as a "market machinery for testing ideas." This position reflects liberal beliefs that "an enlightened citizenry is a political necessity" and that a "free play of ideas will lead to a citizenry equipped to choose the best possible men and policies" (Wills, 1979: 316).

There were two particular attractions within the Lerner thesis that made it seem useful and especially relevant to Third World nations. First of all it strove to unite micro- and macro-levels of development theory. At the macro-level, Lerner and others could discuss the interrelationships among urbanization, education (literacy), communication, and national development. At the micro-level, they argued to have found a process that takes individuals from a traditional to a modern worldview. This modern worldview was reflected by increased powers of empathy (Lerner, 1964: 49–54) and/or the "cognitive flexibility" that allows one to accept change and overcome the "trauma level" which comes with rapid change due to modernization (Frey, 1973: 404).

The second attraction of this thesis for development strategies in the Third World was its recognition of the unique political context of many such nations. LDCs are commonly divided by ethnic differences. Lerner and others argued that certain kinds of communication can help to increase levels of political participation, thereby promoting a sense of national (as opposed to subnational) identification, a belief in the legitimacy of the central government and trust and consensus among ethnic groups. Mass media would be used to promote feelings of trust and to help overcome the tendency of ethnic groups to "refuse to accept the electoral victory of another ethnic coalition because they suspect its intentions." Mass media are also necessary in these states to promote the political cooperation required for establishing national systems of defense, taxation, and welfare. Mass media help to build the consensus necessary to create a single nation from "previously isolated or uncoordinated elements of the traditional society" (Frey, 1973: 381-382).

There are two key elements for the successful operation of the process which the Lerner thesis describes. One is information of a particular kind. The other is a particular mechanism for disseminating that information. The information required shares all the characteristics of news as a commodity discussed earlier. It is information which has its contents determined by the demands of the marketplace. It is concerned more with raw facts than with interpretations of those facts. The key mechanisms for disseminating this information are Western forms of mass media. Lerner (1964), Huntington (1968), and Deutsch (1961) have all made Western mass media the primary tool in their theories of social mobilization. According to Lerner, increased urbanization leads to increased literacy. But these trends create political and economic development through the intervening process of media use (and only by way of media use, according to McCrone and Cnudde, 1967). It is through media use that empathy and cognitive flexibility are developed. It is mass media that "provide a window to a larger and more stimulating world" (Frey, 1973: 404). Media use is said to stimulate economic development by creating a more productive workforce and by increasing individual initiative. It is media use which, according to Lerner, also induces increased political development (i.e., participation such as voting).

Development planning which is based on the Lerner thesis, and which therefore looks to Western mass media as one key to modernization, tends to rely heavily upon Western communication hardware. Films, radio and television programming, and, most importantly, the latest in high-tech hardware are seen as the quickest way for "backward" LDCs to leap into the modern communication age (Davison, 1965: 139). The latest in Western technology (e.g., the direct broadcast satellite [DBS]) is recommended by Lerner and his followers to LDCs wishing to modernize. Unfortunately such recommendations are usually made with little or no evaluation of their advisability given the severe logistical and resource problems of most LDCs.[4]

One would expect the Lerner thesis, given its reliance on information as a commodity and its stress on Western technologies, to offer plans for Third World development along the lines of the Western model. After all, in a free market of ideas, the best ideas are supposed to win out. The past has proved to many in the West that the product of this process of "intellectual Darwinism" (Wills, 1979: 317) are the ideas and ways of Western societies. These are the models that "rational" Third World nations must emulate, if they want to modernize. According to this logic, if Western nations are the most highly developed states, then Western means of development must be best.

Yet many problems of both a practical and theoretical nature have arisen during attempts to apply the Lerner thesis to an understanding of development in the Third World. These problems are best understood in light of a second theory of communication and development, a theory that stands in direct contrast to the Lerner thesis. This is structural theory.

The Structural Thesis

Theories of development that have come out of the structuralist and *dependencia* schools are, in large part, a product of or a reaction to the failing of early postwar attempts at development. The continued hardships and poverty of Third World nations has led these critics to see dependency as the primary source of current Third World problems. Above all else, dependency by LDCs on Western goods, Western-controlled markets, Western tastes, and Western cultures is the condition which allegedly "explains" the continuing dilemmas faced by Third World nations seeking modernization.

Structuralists like Galtung and Schiller have argued that reliance by LDCs on Western mass media and Western sources of information are prime—even paradigmatic—examples of this state of dependency. These authors want to see the Third World break out of this condition of dependency by relying more upon its own resources. However, they also argue that such a feat is not possible within the context of the current system of international communication. Hence their support for radically new orders of international relations.

The structuralists offer what is essentially a Marcusean critique of the Western arguments favoring a free flow of international news and information. Like Marx and Herbert Marcuse, they would charge that bourgeois liberties create a state of freedom in which the powerful are free to dominate the weak. The free flow is seen as an ideological mask that allows the Big Four (AFP, AP, Reuters, UPI) to dominate the market in international news. LDCs are required to rely heavily upon the Big Four for news, thereby allegedly increasing their dependency on the West.

To break out of this pernicious cycle, structuralists argue that each LDC needs more control over the kinds of news and information it receives. Each nation must be allowed more control to decide for itself what its people need to know. They agree with Lerner and others that political and economic development must be pursued through communication policies designed to educate the population and promote a sense of national identification. However, structuralists see an equal need for Third World nations to rely more on indigenous resources and low-tech communication hardware. Schiller sees mimeographs as more in tune with the needs and resources of LDCs than is a communication satellite (1976: 60–67). Instead of recommending the importation of costly and advanced foreign technologies, those who believe that "relevance is beautiful" prefer use of traditional communication within LDCs as being more practical and efficient. The chief of communication for the United Nations International Children's Fund (Unicef), Revi Tuluhungwa, is fond of one example in which employment of traditional modes of spreading information increased the effectiveness of a health education program more than five times over.[5]

Like Lerner and his followers, the structuralists also want to employ communication policies to increase political consensus in LDCs, but the latter group believes that such a task requires governmental controls on media rather than a free market of ideas. Guidelines that reduce that portion of news reports which may serve to divide ethnic groups and instead concentrate on news that concerns progress and successes in national development are necessary (according to this account). Media controls are also said to be necessary for the protection of indigenous cultures. Structuralists argue that a free market in news promotes the demonstration effect, thereby undermining such cultures.

Structural theories of development eschew news and information as commodities in favor of information in the form of a social good. Such theories recommend techniques of developmental journalism to create a political consensus and ensure cultural autonomy. The general aim of structural theory is to create development in a form which is unique to the Third World. They would take from the Western model only that which is necessary and useful. By integrating these Western traits into more traditional cultural modes, they hope to stimulate development which is more relevant to each LDC's unique heritage and pre-modern ways of life.

Two Sets of Testable Hypotheses

Each theory of communication and development has produced a set of testable hypotheses. Partially because the Lerner thesis was articulated and expanded long before the structural thesis, the implications of the former have been researched to a much greater extent than those of the latter. If the Lerner thesis is correct, certain relationships will hold true between the processes of development (e.g., urbanization, communication) in Third World states. Furthermore, if this thesis is valid, one would also expect certain trends to hold among groups of LDCs. On the basis of the Lerner thesis, one would expect to find that developing nations with free markets in news and information also tend to be those nations which are more politically and economically developed.

On the other hand, if the structural thesis is more valid, those nations that regulate closely the inflows of foreign news and information will also tend to be the nations which are most successful at maintaining their political stability and developing a strong sense of national identification. These same nations would also tend to be those that are least dependent on the West both economically and culturally. If nations with a highly regulated media were found to be those nations with greater political stability and less dependence, this fact would tend to support the structuralist's argument. It would also tend to refute parts of the free flow arguments. Conversely, if nations with free markets in news and information were also found to be more advanced politically and economically, this fact would tend to support the Lerner thesis (free flow arguments) and tend to deny the validity of at least part of the structural thesis.

The first set of hypotheses—those of the Lerner thesis—have been investigated by Alker, Frey, Lerner, McCrone and Cnudde, Ruggles, Schramm, and Winham (see Frey, 1973 for an overview). The results of these studies have been conflicting and inconclusive. Lerner's theoretical link between literacy and political development has been supported by one study (Alker, 1966) and questioned by another (McCrone and Cnudde, 1967). The same is true of the link postulated by Lerner between literacy and mass media use (Frey, 1973: 416).

At another level, the basic assumptions of the theory have been called into question. Its bias toward a unilinear, mechanistic view of history and development has been severely criticized. A theory that postulates "progress" from traditional to transitional to modern "stages" of development seems much more tenuous today, in light of numerous failures and setbacks, than it must have been twenty or twenty-five years ago. The change in values at the micro-level that is supposed to come about through urbanization has also been put into doubt by studies of Latin America (see Martz, 1971). In that region one finds examples of nations in which increases in the indicators of Lerner's model (e.g., media use) are not associated with the political development predicted by the model. The Latin American experience also stands as a reminder that, by no means, do economic and political development always go hand in hand, as is postulated by the Lerner thesis.

The second set of theoretical claims—those of the structural thesis— remain virtually untested. The untested nature of structuralism is probably due in large part to the overtly ideological nature of this theory. Schiller and others seem to assume that their arguments are correct and feel little need to demonstrate their validity through empirical testing. Western conservatives, on the other hand, seem to assume the invalidity of this theory due to its ideological underpinnings. A critical examination reveals that neither theory has been proved conclusively, and the structural thesis is as much in need of testing as was its predecessor. Structuralism may be better able to explain development in the Third World than was the Lerner thesis, or it may be badly flawed and in need of refinement and overhaul, as was the case with the Lerner thesis. Such is the task of the remainder of this study.

Testing the structural thesis will also serve to test parts of the Lerner thesis, at least indirectly. Through several series of tests, quantitative analyses will allow for numerous opportunities to confirm or refute structural claims. If nothing is found after all these various tests are run, then there is more than prima facie evidence to indicate that structural arguments won't hold water. This in turn would tend to support those parts of the Lerner thesis (discussed above) on the points at which these two directly contradict each other.

NOTES

1. Kenya recently threatened to expel as many as 100 foreign (mostly Western) correspondents after charging American and Scandinavian presses with conducting smear campaigns. This is especially disturbing, given the fact that more Western correspondents are based in Nairobi than in any other place in sub-Saharan Africa (*New York Times*, 16 September, 1987). It is also an indication that previously moderate LDCs, like Kenya, which have provided press freedom in the past are falling in behind the more radical policies preferred by Zimbabwe and others.

2. My historical arguments rely on three principal sources: Desmond's three-volume history of international news; Smith's *Geopolitics of Information*; and Righter's *Whose News?*

3. Somavia, a member of the MacBride Commission from Chile, is one of the leading theorists of news as a social good. His work is reviewed in Righter, pp. 107–109, and in Smith, pp. 101–103.

4. According to Bella Mody, who did the governmental study of the social impact of a DBS project in India, the question of whether it made sense to use such a sophisticated technology in a nation as poor as India was never raised. Mody made these comments at a 1984 colloquium on communication and Third World development at the University of Iowa.

5. At the same colloquium, Tuluhungwa said that an African health program went from 15 percent to 85 percent effectiveness simply by turning to the traditional means of communication (that already existed in the area) in order to inform the public of the project.

3

Flows of News and Broadcasting to the Third World

COMMUNICATION IN DEVELOPING NATIONS

Communication in less developed countries (LDCs) is constrained by economic, educational and demographic factors. Because financial resources are scarce, government ownership of news media and the national press is the rule (Blake, 1979: 225; Davison, 1965: 137). Low literacy rates are also common—rates of 25 percent to 30 percent are considered "high." Low levels of literacy mean that broadcast media are of greater importance for reaching the masses than is the printed word (Davison, 1965: 133; Kurian, 1982: 570; Schramm, 1964). Radio, like the press, is usually government-owned. Small radio stations and newspapers, employing local dialects, usually operate at a loss and require public funds (Blake, 1979: 225). Governments then find that they may be able to use the media to increase the interests of the masses, and to rally popular support for national movements (Davison, 1965: 149).

It was only recently that communication specialists from the West realized the importance of traditional forms of communication in the Third World (Bhattacharya, 1976: 61). Integration of the folk media (e.g., word of mouth, ceremony, dance, song) with more modern mass communication technologies, where before there had been "little relationship between the two systems," promises to increase the effectiveness of national communication policies while, at the same time, reducing some of the economic burdens (Blake, 1979: 222; Davison, 1965: 136–146; see also Martin's discussion of the unique nature of mass media in LDCs as contrasted with Western models, 1983: 191–194; and Revi Tuluhungwa's example discussed in Chapter Two).

At the international level, the political context for Third World com-

Table 3.1:
The Flow of Broadcasting to the Third World

MEDIUM	TOTAL HOURS	IMPORTED	% IMPORTED
Radio & TV	7,159,129	250,091	4%
Radio (alone)	6,749,677	117,344	2%
TV (alone)	409,452	132,747	32%

source: Unesco, 1978

munication has been set by a number of charges made by nonaligned diplomats who advocate the New World Information Order (NWIO), and by structural theorists of international communication such as Johan Galtung and Herbert Schiller. These groups believe that global imbalances create a condition of informational dependency by the South on the North in the areas of news and broadcasting. This alleged dependency is made worse by what NWIO supporters see as biased and sensationalist reporting of LDCs by Western correspondents (Masmoudi, 1979). Finally, structural theorists charge that international communications follow neocolonial patterns and allow for domination of the Third World by the Western industrialized nations (Becker et al., 1986; Galtung, 1980; Schiller, 1976). These charges—regarding imbalances, biased reporting, and a neocolonial structure—prompt the research presented here. Examination of Unesco data on international broadcasting and a study of news flows in Africa and Latin America allow for an assessment of the validity of these claims.

INTERNATIONAL BROADCASTING AND THE THIRD WORLD

Critics of the current system of international communication have charged that the Third World is dependent on the West for radio and television programming. They go on to criticize Western broadcasting for being, at best, superfluous to the national needs of the LDCs. At worst, such programming is condemned as constituting "subversive elements from outside" which "perform disruptive communication" within developing nations (Blake, 1979: 226). Blake derides such shows as "Mission Impossible" and "The Beverly Hillbillies" (popular in Sierra Leone) and points out their lack of relevance to African national development (p. 227). Dependency on Western broadcasting is also said to create a whole host of cultural, economic, and law-and-order problems for developing nations due to the demonstration effect (see Chapter Four).

Table 3.1 contains data taken from Unesco[1] for total hours of radio and television broadcasting in forty-three developing nations during the 1960s

Table 3.2:
Average Broadcasting in Forty-three Developing Nations

MEDIUM	HOURS
Television	15,523
Radio	434,675
	450,198

Average Broadcasting Imported = 20.13%

source: Unesco, 1978

and 1970s.[2] The data have been broken down according to that amount which is produced domestically as opposed to that which is imported. Table 3.2 presents the mean values for these nations, as well as the average percentage of total broadcasting which is imported: 20.13 percent.

As one can see from Tables 3.1 and 3.2, these Third World nations are somewhat dependent upon the West for their television programming. Nearly one-third of all television broadcasting is imported. Because the nations which export television programming are almost exclusively Western, it is safe to assume that most of this imported media does come from the West (McPhail, 1987).

In that medium generally recognized by mass communication experts to be the most influential in developing nations (Schramm, 1964), only a very small percentage of radio broadcasting is imported. Only 2 percent of all radio programming in developing nations comes from outside (possibly Western) sources. Therefore, if charges of an imbalance in broadcasting are valid to any extent, it is only in the area of television programming. LDCs produce nearly all of their own radio programming, and even a full two-thirds of all television shows are produced within the developing nations themselves.

It seems that charges of an imbalance in international communication, when discussing broadcasting, are vastly overstated. To see if these charges have any greater justification in regard to international news reporting, a more detailed discussion of news flows in the Third World is in order.

THE FLOW OF NEWS TO THE THIRD WORLD

The Papers

The data presented in the remainder of this chapter are taken from three English-language African dailies—the *Daily Nation* (Nairobi, Kenya); the Zimbabwe *Herald*, and the *Times of Zambia*—and three Latin American dailies—*Excelsior* (Mexico City), *La Nacion*, and *La Prensa* (both from Buenos Aires). I have selected from each nation the publication with either the largest daily circulation (ranging from 235,000 to 65,000) and/or papers which are ranked by Kurian as being the "most influential" (1982: 89, 630). Each also ranks among the largest, in terms of circulation, in its respective region. All six papers cater primarily to urban elites, with little or no rural circulation (Kurian, 1982). This means that these papers are read by groups within developing nations that the demonstration effect is said to influence (Galtung, 1979). That is, these are among the primary sources of daily news and information for that group (elites) which is allegedly stimulated by Western media to desire a more westernized culture and more Western-style goods.

These particular dailies were sampled for a number of reasons. They are among the few papers from the nonaligned world that consistently identify the sources of their news stories in the byline (an important consideration for reasons which will soon become apparent). They also represent both government-owned and independent presses. The *Herald* and *Times* are in the former category, the *Daily Nation* and the American dailies are in the latter.

There are two additional considerations that make the African dailies particularly important for my purposes. First, Black Africa is a region neglected in most prior news flow studies (Harris, 1981a; Harris et al., 1982; IPI, 1953; Schramm and Atwood, 1981; Stevenson and Cole, 1980; Stevenson and Shaw, 1984; Rogers and Schement, 1984). Furthermore, news flows in this part of Africa represent a best-case test[3] of the structuralist's charge that international communication is neocolonial (Galtung, 1979; McPhail, 1987; Schiller, 1976). Nations in this area are the countries which, as a group, have received their independence most recently. If the patterns of communication that were established during the age of imperialism (see Chapter Two) persist to this day, then evidence of that fact is most likely to remain in sub-Saharan Africa.

Africa is a region in which many colonial powers (e.g., Belgium, Britain, France, Germany, Portugal) had established strongholds of suzerainty. If ex-colonial powers still control information flows in and out of their former colonies (as specified by structural theory), evidence of such a trend is most likely to show up in news reports from Africa and in news reported within Africa. Should the structuralists' claims be correct, one would expect news from former British colonies to be carried via Reuters, news regarding former French colonies via the Agence France Presse (AFP), and so forth. The best way to test this thesis is to study international news of Africa as carried in the African press. If something like informational spheres of influence do exist, this is the most likely place to find evidence of it.

The African papers, published in a European language, served residents of European extraction in the days before independence (Kurian, 1982).

Hence, if any local newspapers are linked to the existing information order in a neoimperial manner, it should be these. Evidence of the sorts of things that structuralists look for (e.g., Galtung's alleged link between the news interests of Center and Periphery elites) should be most readily apparent in these particular publications.[4]

On the other hand, Latin American states have enjoyed their independence from colonialism longer than any other region of the Third World. This is another geographic area which is also underrepresented in prior news flow studies. Therefore, a focus on these two regions not only fills in some of the gaps in the prior literature, but it also gives us samples that reflect some of the diversity of the Third World's colonial experience.

The Samples

The data presented are taken from five issues of each of the three major African dailies during 1984, five issues of each African paper for 1985, and four issues of each Latin American publication for 1985 (for a total of forty-two issues). A grand total of 1,598 stories regarding international affairs (with roughly half coming from each region) was coded from stratified samples. Prior news flow studies encountered difficulties because their samples were often skewed toward coverage of one or two major events (see, for example, Schramm, 1980: 613). Because studies by Harris, the International Press Institute, Schramm, and others took their samples from only one week (or at most one month) of the year, the distribution of news items was commonly dominated by one or two recurring stories. This fact casts doubts upon the validity of generalizing from such samples. Schramm's influential study of Asian media employs a sample that is admitted to be unique in some respects (i.e., coverage of an airline disaster dominated international news) (1980: 613). Therefore, that sample is less representative of average news coverage than might be desired.

In this sampling, such problems are avoided by drawing on a more representative distribution of the Third World press. Papers were sampled from a six-month time period.[5] By using a random sample from all available issues for a larger time-frame—random with the exception that no two issues were taken from the same week—a more balanced and accurate portrayal of the nonaligned press is the result. It is more representative due to the fact that it is not skewed by one or two major events, and is, therefore, closer to the norm for all reporting.

Each story in the sample was coded for the paper and date of publication, the wire service carrying the story,[6] the nation and region covered in the story, the theme, the total column-inches and lines for the story, the column-inches/lines devoted to spot news, and column-inches/lines for developmental news.

Spot news is generally regarded as raw facts about diplomacy, wars, crime, unrest, and disasters. Developmental news is not just news about modernization or other forms of development. The style known as developmental journalism attempts to imbue all news stories with the links between a raw data-event and projects of economic or political modernization. Developmental journalism also addresses the historical background and long-range implications of an isolated event (Aggarwala, 1979; see also the discussion of news as a social good in Chapter Two). The developmental approach to reporting is illustrated by the following item taken from the Zambian *Times* (31 January, 1985) with the caption "Disease Kills 79 Tanzanians":

(Nairobi, Wednesday). A total of 79 people have died from cholera and dysentery in the Lindi region of southern Tanzania in the last two months.

Radio Tanzania, monitored here, quoted a Lindi medical official as saying that cholera claimed the lives of 54 people in the region between December 12 and January 28, while 18 others were hospitalised in the same period.

The official said the dysentery situation in the region was still critical and that 40 people had been hospitalised so far with the disease.

Malawi's bilharzia eradication pilot programme mounted by the ministry of health three years ago has been cited by the World Health Organization as one of the most successful efforts in this area being carried out today in the Third World.

In a report from Geneva, the widely read international English journal, INTERNATIONAL HERALD TRIBUNE, published in Dakar, quoted WHO as saying that Malawi, whose 16.6 per cent of the population who had been affected before the pilot programme began, had now managed to reduce the rate to 12 per cent.

Sudan was the other African country cited as having succeeded in reducing the infection rate to 14 per cent. (Zana/Pana.)

Here we have a clear example of the contrast between spot and developmental news, as well as a good illustration of how the developmental style tries to merge aspects of both types of news into a single report. The first three paragraphs are of the spot news variety. A minor crisis having to do with a problem common to many developing nations is reported in brief. Such reports of disease and epidemics in LDCs are not uncommon in the press here in the United States. What sets this item apart from similar treatments in the Western media is the second half of the report. The last three paragraphs go on to detail cases in which similar problems have been successfully addressed in other parts of the Third World. Therefore, the item as a whole not only presents a more balanced picture of public health in Africa, but it also provides a sharing of information between LDCs that may be used to their mutual benefit. A Western newspaper would be most likely to carry only the first half of this item, without the further discussion that draws connections from the minor crisis to related events of interest for those directly involved.

The report above was coded as part spot news (three paragraphs) and part developmental news. Once the data had been gathered in this way, the analysis was divided according to the three research questions discussed below: imbalances in news flows; differences in news reporting between the Big Four transnational news agencies and the local or regional nonaligned agencies; and the structure of international news flows.

IMBALANCES IN NEWS FLOWS?

The discussion has already dealt with the extent to which an imbalance may exist in international flows of broadcasting. It was shown that this term is accurate only if it is used to characterize television programming. It is possible to address the same theme by using the study of African and Latin American news flows; looking specifically at the nature of the news reported, the sources of the news items, and the areas covered in those news items.

When NWIO advocates and structuralists speak of an imbalance, they may be referring to one of two things. At times they are speaking of an imbalance in the form of dependency: a heavy reliance by LDCs on the Western news agencies. At other times they are referring to a lack of coverage about the Third World by Western wire services and dailies, and, as a result, an alleged tendency for Western news practices to be copied in the Third World. We could call this an imbalance in the form of journalistic westernization. The two forms of imbalance are also interrelated. The imbalance of media dependency is said to lead to the homogenization of the world's presses. As LDCs are bombarded by media fare from the West, they come to see the world through Western eyes and adopt Western values. To evaluate charges of an imbalance fairly, one must look at both areas (e.g., dependency, westernization).

Looking at the latter form of imbalance (westernized media), the first question one might pose is whether international news is treated any differently in the Third World press than it is in the West. Table 3.3 shows that these dailies devoted between 11 percent and 52 percent of all news to reports on international affairs, with average coverage ranging from 23 percent to 39 percent. Figures for average coverage of interstate news are close to those of Schramm's study in Asia (18 percent to 28 percent) and Pinch's 1978 study of the *New York Times*, *Washington Post*, and the *Los Angeles Times* (20 percent to 30 percent). Note that the averages for Africa increase from 1984 to 1985, indicating a rising interest in international affairs over that period. Average international coverage in the 1985 Latin American press is greater than that of Africa for 1984, but roughly equivalent to African dailies for 1985.

When looking at the regions covered in the Southern presses (see Table 3.4 for Third World versus non–Third World coverage), one finds, again,

Table 3.3:
Percentage of All News for International Reporting

	AFRICA					LATIN AMERICA		
D. Nation		Herald		Times		Excelsior	La Nacion	La Prensa
1984/85		84/85		84/85		1985	1985	1985

ISSUE								
1.	15%	33%	11%	21%	21%	37%	32%	31%	39%
2.	23%	24%	36%	27%	31%	45%	38%	35%	35%
3.	24%	23%	18%	34%	39%	52%	32%	22%	22%
4.	31%	28%	26%	39%	26%	31%	32%	27%	16%
5.	22%	43%	23%	33%	31%	31%			
AVERAGES									
	23%	30%	24%	31%	30%	39%	33%	29%	28%

Table 3.4:
Regions Covered in African and Latin American Presses

	AFRICA				LATIN AMERICA	
	(1984)		(1985)		(1985)	
	N	%	N	%	N	%
REGION						
Africa	197	47%	192	41%	10	1%
Asia	33	8%	62	13%	40	6%
Latin America	13	3%	17	4%	291	42%
Middle East	32	8%	32	7%	21	3%
United States	37	9%	33	7%	137	20%
USSR/E. Europe	11	2%	19	4%	39	6%
Western Europe	89	21%	99	21%	152	22%
Other	8	2%	12	3%	6	1%
Third World	162	39%	182	39%	239	34%
Third W. + Other	122	29%	124	26%	223	32%
Non-Third World	136	32%	163	35%	241	34%

results similar to those of Schramm's (1981: 205) for the Asian press. Each region of the Third World devotes about 40 percent to 45 percent of all international news to the local area, and each region devotes roughly two-thirds of its international coverage to news involving at least one nonaligned nation. As Schramm points out, these results also correlate strongly (and positively) with Big Four coverage (p. 209). Therefore, Third World dailies

Table 3.5:
1,600 News Items According to Topics

	AFRICA (1984)		AFRICA (1985)		LATIN AMERICA (1985)	
Topic	N	%	N	%	N	%
Development	30	7%	28	6%	20	3%
Diplomatic Relations	86	20%	72	15%	101	14%
Disasters	18	4%	29	6%	13	2%
Domestic Politics	38	9%	43	9%	62	9%
Economics	38	9%	35	7%	109	15%
Society, Culture, Science	29	7%	55	12%	104	15%
Sports	70	17%	109	23%	165	23%
Unrest and Crime	74	18%	69	15%	63	9%
War and Military Affairs	37	9%	30	6%	69	10%

in Africa, Asia, and Latin America all show evidence of following the lead of Western papers and Western wire services in focusing on certain regions and countries.

Turning now to the subjects covered, Table 3.5 shows the distribution of news items according to topics. Once again the African and Latin American presses exhibit striking similarities to the Asian and American presses. Of all the stories in these samples, 13 percent to 18 percent focused on economic and political development in the African/Latin American samples, compared with a range of 15 percent to 28 percent for Asian dailies and 14 percent to 25 percent for U.S. dailies. In another area of similarity, 9 percent to 18 percent of the stories in these samples were about crimes and unrest, a paradigm of spot reporting almost identical in range to the results of Schramm (10 percent in Asia) and Pinch (17 percent in U.S. dailies).

On the basis of results such as these, Schramm and Pinch have argued that there is no significant difference between Western papers and Third World dailies when it comes to coverage of developmental news versus coverage of other news. Results from this study, combined with those of the earlier news flow studies, suggest that Asian, African, Latin American, and Western dailies also approximate one another in percentages of news for interstate reporting and in regions covered. These conclusions are shared by many who see little difference between Western and Third World newspapers in general (Stevenson and Cole, 1980; Stevenson, 1981). Findings from this study support the claim that Third World *dailies* treat developmental news much like Western papers do, but as we shall see in the next section, Third World *newswires* treat developmental reports in a significantly different manner than do Western newswires.

As a final consideration addressing imbalances, let us look for evidence

Table 3.6:
Newswires Identified as Sources

	AFRICA			
	(1984)		(1985)	
Wire Service	N	%	N	%
TNNA:				
Agence France Presse	69	16% (23%)	38	9% (13%)
Associated Press	42	10% (14%)	57	13% (19%)
Reuters	110	26% (36%)	87	20% (29%)
United Press International	9	2% (3%)	2	.5% (1%)
NON-TNNA:				
Local/Regional Services	27	7% (9%)	33	8% (11%)
Special Services	4	1% (1%)	13	3% (4%)
Paper's Own Reporter (rather than a wire service)	45	11% (15%)	66	16% (22%)
No Source Identified	114	27%	131	31%

	LATIN AMERICA	
	(1985)	
	N	%
TNNA:		
Agence France Presse	57	10% (11%)
Associated Press	104	18% (19%)
Reuters	19	3% (4%)
United Press International	116	20% (22%)
NON-TNNA:		
Local/Regional Services	158	27% (29%)
Special Services	42	7% (8%)
Paper's Own Reporter	42	7% (8%)
No Source Identified	44	7%

of dependency in the sources of international news. Table 3.6 shows the distribution of the news stories according to sources. Figures in parentheses are percentages of all news stories with identified sources. A tally of all stories shows that 56 percent to 76 percent of all identifiable sources in these six dailies were attributed to the four Western international agencies.[7] We now know that this pattern is repeated in other areas of the Third World, as these results are very close to Schramm's findings of 75 percent for Asian dailies (1980: 597). From these samples we can also see that the African press tends to be more reliant on the Big Four than is Latin

America. The latter region takes more news off of the regional wire services, especially from EFE, the Spanish service, and from IPS, a specialist in developmental news (Giffard: 1985).

Special note should be taken of the totals in Table 3.6 for news supplied to Africa by Reuters and for news to Latin America from AP and UPI. Of all identified newswire stories on international relations, as reported in the Kenyan, Zambian, and Zimbabwean press, 29 percent to 36 percent (the largest single group) came from the British newswire. Recall that each of these nations is also a former British colony. Similarly, 41 percent of all global news in the Latin American press came from the two U.S. TNNAs combined. Of course, Central and South America are often argued to be in the imperial sphere of the United States. Here the evidence suggests that international news flows through neoimperial channels (see below).

African, Asian, Latin American, and Western dailies do show striking similarities in terms of the topics and regions they cover. This is consistent with Galtung's claim that the news media used by Periphery elites follow the same format as the Western media (1979: 165). This is also one of the conditions which NWIO advocates such as Harris (1981b) and Masmoudi (1981) describe as an imbalance: the alleged shaping of the Third World press in the Western mold. In the other area of imbalance—media dependency—the African, Asian, and American surveys show that TNNAs account for between one-half and three-fourths of the foreign reports in the Third World presses. Therefore, we find empirical support to bolster some of the critical allegations that mass media in LDCs are in a dependent state.

TNNA VERSUS THIRD WORLD NEWS AGENCY COVERAGE

Do the Big Four TNNAs (AFP, AP, Reuters, UPI) give biased accounts of Third World news? More specifically, to what extent do reports drawn from TNNAs differ from those taken off of the nonaligned newswires? Critics of Western journalism have frequently charged that reports from TNNAs focus mostly on spot news, forcing Third World editors to turn to national and regional nonaligned news agencies for developmental news and alternative news values.

Table 3.7 divides the news items according to source: TNNA, versus national and regional (nonaligned) services, versus local correspondents and stringers. Coverage from each source is further broken down according to subject matter. The categories of Diplomatic Relations, War, and Crime and Unrest (spot news categories) rank high for reports drawn from the TNNAs. Conversely, developmental news ranks significantly higher, in terms of percentages, for both national/regional newswires and local coverage. Obviously the tendency is for stories with Big Four bylines to focus

Table 3.7:
Topics According to Source (Percentages)

	DIPLOMATIC RELATIONS	CRIME & UNREST	WARS & MILITARY	DISASTER	DEVELOPMENT
SAMPLE =	A84/A85	A84/A85	A84/A85	A84/A85	A84/A85
AFP	16/11%	35/21%	13/18%	4/ 5%	6/ 0%
AP	19/14%	17/28%	17/ 2%	10/ 9%	2/ 5%
Reuters	27/20%	19/15%	14/ 9%	4/ 6%	6/ 2%
UPI	22/ 0%	22/50%	11/ 0%	0/ 0%	0/ 0%
National/ Regional	20/24%	16/ 6%	12/ 3%	8/21%	20/15%
Paper's Reporter	29/17%	4/ 3%	2/ 3%	0/ 3%	27/23%
SAMPLE =	LA85	LA85	LA85	LA85	LA85
AFP	11%	21%	0%	4%	0%
AP	12%	14%	7%	5%	1%
Reuters	21%	10%	21%	5%	5%
UPI	13%	14%	14%	1%	1%
National/ Regional	15%	3%	7%	0%	8%
Paper's Reporter	18%	5%	13%	0%	5%

A84 = Africa, 1984
A85 = Africa, 1985
LA85 = Latin America, 1985

on diplomacy and crime and unrest, while stories from nonaligned agencies are relatively more apt to focus on development (in addition to international diplomacy).

Table 3.8 presents a slightly more sophisticated treatment of the same question. Here the columns are divided into TNNA (Big Four) news sources and non-TNNA sources (national or regional newswires and local correspondents). The row of Spot News contains all stories coded originally as diplomacy, unrest and crime, domestic politics (from other nations), wars, or disasters. Developmental reports are only those in which either the subject was one of national modernization or over half of the item was devoted to the developmental journalistic style (see above). The category of Other contains mostly social, cultural, or scientific news and a few human interest stories. Sports news was not included in this table.

Cross-tabular analysis of TNNA versus non-TNNA news sources shows

Table 3.8:
Spot News Versus Developmental Reporting

AFRICA (1984)

	TNNA	LOCAL-REGIONAL
SPOT NEWS	N = 194 (85%)	N = 41 (57%)
DEVELOPMENTAL REPORTS	N = 11 (5%)	N = 17 (24%)
OTHER	N = 24 (10%)	N = 14 (19%)
TOTALS	229 (100%)	72 (100%)

Chi-square = 29.72; significant at less than .001 level

AFRICA (1985)

	TNNA	LOCAL-REGIONAL
SPOT NEWS	N = 134 (73%)	N = 54 (55%)
DEV. NEWS	N = 5 (3%)	N = 20 (20%)
OTHER	N = 45 (24%)	N = 25 (25%)
TOTALS	184 (100%)	99 (100%)

Chi-square = 25.53; significant at less than .001

LATIN AMERICA (1985)

	TNNA	LOCAL-REGIONAL
SPOT NEWS	N = 173 (59%)	N = 161 (55%)
DEV. NEWS	N = 3 (1%)	N = 14 (5%)
OTHER	N = 119 (40%)	N = 115 (40%)
TOTALS	295 (100%)	290 (100%)

Chi-square = 7.57; significant at .02

D.F. = 2

that there is a statistically significant difference between reports taken from the two. The chi-square tests show that the probability of there being no relationship between news source and subject matter is less than .05 for all three samples. Again, the clear trend is for stories with a TNNA byline to center on spot news, while those with a nonaligned news service byline

Table 3.9:
Mean Values for Developmental Reports—Analysis of Variance (ANOVA)

AFRICA (1984) MEANS			ANOVA			
	TNNA	Non-TNNA		D.F.	F-Ratio	Significance
Total Lines	3.38	25.39	Between Within	1 300	31.41	.000*
Total Inches	.43	4.65	Between Within	1 300	27.28	.000*
AFRICA (1985) MEANS			ANOVA			
	TNNA	Non-TNNA		D.F.	F-Ratio	Significance
Total Lines	2.70	11.20	Between Within	1 323	13.10	.000*
Total Inches	.53	1.80	Between Within	1 323	8.46	.003
LATIN AMERICA (1985) MEANS			ANOVA			
	TNNA	Non-TNNA		D.F.	F-Ratio	Significance
Total Lines	2.80	16.60	Between Within	1 619	13.37	.000*
Total Inches	.41	2.30	Between Within	1 619	13.65	.000*

* = significant at less than the .001 level

display a greater interest in developmental news. But what of those developmental reports that are taken off of the TNNA newswires? Table 3.9 compares the mean values for length of developmental reports taken from TNNAs with the mean values of those taken from non-TNNA news services.

Reports taken from nonaligned news services are not only more likely to cover developmental news (as per Table 3.8), but they also go into much greater detail in their developmental reports (as per Table 3.9). Average length of a developmental news item from a Third World source is at least four times greater than that of a TNNA story about development. ANOVA (analysis of variance) tests comparing the mean values for developmental reports acquired from the two types of news sources show that there is a statistically significant difference in both total column-inches and total lines at less than the .01 level for all three samples. Not only do the articles which cite the nonaligned agencies as sources focus more on developmental news than those citing TNNAs, but they also go into the subject of development at much greater length and in more detail.

DOES INTERNATIONAL COMMUNICATION EXHIBIT A NEOCOLONIAL STRUCTURE?

The last question to be addressed by this news flow study is the one which is most central to the structuralists' views. The claim is repeatedly made that international communication is a prime—even paradigmatic—example of the neoimperial structure of world affairs. If one were to find clear evidence of structural imperialism in the area of communication, this fact would tend to support the claim of Galtung and others that a feudal structure characterizes North-South relations in general. On the other hand, if the structural view of communication were found to be inaccurate, then structural theory in general would be seriously undermined.

The testing of structural theories of international relations has itself become a controversial issue. Proof of the empirical validity of such "critical" theories is said to be demonstrated by their capacity to transform the international system (Cox, 1986). Theorists of dependency and structuralism have claimed that validation of their work can be found only in its relative ability to promote new forms of political action (Galtung, 1980: Chapter 9) and socio-economic organization (Cardoso and Faletto, 1979: xiv). Cardoso and Faletto decry past attempts at empirical testing as being efforts to quantify what may be inherently unquantifiable (1979: xii). Furthermore, the neocolonial interaction structure of information flows is something which has already been "amply demonstrated" in Galtung's view (1980: 129), although he cites no empirical studies to support this point.

Quantitative studies of international communication have been few and far between (for recent efforts see Cioffi-Revilla et al., 1987; Stevenson and Shaw, 1984). Mass communication researchers who purport to have tested structural theory have been particularly unsophisticated in their analyses, with a clear tendency to oversimplify structural claims before proceeding to "refute" them (Haynes, 1984; Link, 1984). Haynes believes that he can demonstrate the invalidity of structural thought by calling our attention to the fact that the Latin American press carries news about other Third World regions (i.e., interactions exist between the Peripheral states). Any Periphery-to-Periphery (horizontal) linkages of this sort, according to Haynes, refute Galtung's claim that neocolonial information flows always follow a Center-to-Periphery (vertical) structure. However, one cannot hope to counter structural claims with evidence as meager as this.

What Galtung is trying to show us is that flows from one region of the Periphery to another must normally be channeled through the Center (e.g.,

Table 3.10:
Regions Covered According to Their Colonial History

	AFRICA				LATIN AMERICA	
	1984		1985		1985	
	N	%	N	%	N	%
IMPERIAL POWER						
France	48	12%	24	8%	14	4%
United Kingdom	236	56%	227	76%	28	8%
United States	50	12%	19	6%	301	85%
More Than One	33	8%	10	3%	6	2%
West European (Not UK or France)	30	7%	10	3%	4	1%
Other or None	23	5%	9	3%	2	.5%

the West), which acts as the intermediary for all economic sectors of the Periphery (and profits nicely in the bargain). If news from former British colonies comes to Africa and South America through Reuters (the British service), and events in former French colonies are reported primarily by AFP (the French agency), while news from within the U.S. sphere of influence comes mainly via AP or UPI, one would find strong evidence to support the notion of feudal, Periphery-to-Center-to-Periphery (vertical) interaction patterns. Such structures would be consistent with Haynes' findings, yet they would also stand as confirmation of Galtung's thought. Perhaps Haynes did not consider this possibility.

On the other hand, there is no reason one should be expected to accept structural theses as true a priori (as NWIO advocates tend to do); and structural theory deserves no special dispensation from the scientific tasks of empirical validation and critical evaluation. Therefore, even if one is sympathetic to the position that structuralism has been unjustly slighted and inadequately comprehended by the mainstream of international relations literature, nevertheless it must be acknowledged that new steps need to be taken toward empirically testing this school of thought.

To state the structural thesis in its broadest form, the claim is that British multinational corporations (MNCs) are still dominant in the political economies of former British colonies, French MNCs hold a similar position in former French colonies, and U.S. MNCs hold dominance in areas historically under U.S. hegemony. The multinationals of the news industry, the TNNAs, are cited as clear examples of this trend. Tables 3.10 and 3.11 present data from the news flow study relevant to these claims.

Simple extensions of the prior data (see Table 3.10) show that, when looking at regions covered in international reports carried in the major dailies of three former British colonies (Kenya, Zambia, Zimbabwe), one-

Table 3.11:
News Flows as Compared with Imperial Hegemony

WIRE SERVICE	IMPERIAL POWER FOR NATION/REGION IN REPORT			
	UNITED STATES	UNITED KINGDOM	FRANCE	OTHER
US	N = 95 (71%)	N = 60 (29%)	N = 14 (25%)	N = 8 (26%)
BRITISH	N = 16 (12%)	N = 99 (48%)	N = 17 (31%)	N = 11 (35%)
FRENCH	N = 23 (17%)	N = 46 (23%)	N = 23 (44%)	N = 12 (39%)
TOTALS	134 (100%)	205 (100%)	54 (100%)	31 (100%)

Chi-square = 84.96; significant at less than the .001 level

D.F. = 6

half to three-fourths of the news covers other nations or regions which were also formerly under British imperial control. In Latin America, an area widely accepted to be part of the U.S. sphere of influence, a full 85 percent of all international news concerns this and other regions under American hegemony.[8] However, these facts do not necessarily indicate neocolonial spheres of informational influence. It could be that commonalities of interest and common problems make these states more interested in one another, not to mention the fact that most of their immediate neighbors have had the same colonial master.

Table 3.11 presents information that more directly addresses this question. Each news item was coded for the former colonial ruler of the nation or region covered in the report. Each story was also coded for the nationality of the TNNA (if any) carrying the report. The association of former imperial power in the area to nationality of TNNA reporting from the area was then evaluated.

It is true that Latin America and Africa carry a great deal of news about LDCs from beyond their own region (as Haynes has shown). However, from Table 3.11 we see that these flows clearly follow a vertical structure. Seventy-one percent of all news about areas formerly or currently under U.S. hegemony comes to the South via AP and UPI (combined). This pattern is repeated in regions historically dominated by England or France. Almost half of the stories about areas which have been part of the vast

British empire have been channeled to the six papers in this study by Reuters. A comparable figure also holds for the French imperial domain (44 percent). Therefore, when we look beneath the surface appearances of the Third World press, when we look beyond the mere fact of which regions are covered, and compare the sources of international news to the geopolitics of colonialism, we find that a vertical flow does characterize news inputs into the media of the developing world. It appears that the legacy of the nineteenth-century Ring Combination, the first global communication cartel, (see Chapter Two) reaches far into contemporary international relations.

Concluding remarks for this chapter assess the overall implications of this work for the three research questions at hand.

CONCLUSIONS

In regard to imbalances in international information flows, this study shows Third World nations to be dependent to some extent on Western television programming, but almost self-sufficient in the more important area of radio broadcasting (more important due to the heavy reliance on radio and the relative paucity of television in LDCs). In the area of news media, Third World dailies generally show close similarities to U.S. "prestige" dailies in regard to the geographic areas and topics covered. These findings are consistent with prior news flow studies, and point to an imbalance in the form of Western news values being replicated in the major dailies of the South. In addition, there is an imbalance to the extent that 56 percent to 76 percent of the international news reports carrying a byline in the Latin American and African presses came from a TNNA, indicating a continued reliance on the Western newswires.

In regard to biased reporting, stories in this sample taken from TNNAs do focus more on spot reports of diplomacy, unrest and crime, and disasters. Local and regional nonaligned services are more concerned with developmental news. When one looks at developmental reports in particular, the finding is that articles from the nonaligned agencies deal more in in-depth reporting than do those taken from the TNNAs. Therefore, local and regional services provide usable information to Third World editors which is different from that of the Big Four in this important respect. If editors want in-depth developmental coverage they will find that it is not generally available from the TNNAs and they must go elsewhere to national or regional services, or have their reporters produce such reports on their own. Clearly, the claim by Stevenson and Cole (1980: 13) that "Western agencies ... set the agenda for [Third World] media at the level of influencing what ... topics get covered" is questionable. Furthermore, to assume, as Merrill does, that "one Third World country is not interested in development news of another Third World country" (1981: 156) would also be a mistake.

On the other hand, one of Stevenson's later points is well taken. Stevenson argues, and this study confirms, that Third World dailies do not lack for informational alternatives to the TNNAs (1981: 5). Western news agencies do not have anything like a stranglehold on the news supplied to Southern papers, as some of the more extreme structuralists would seem to imply. There does appear to be, however, a clear "shortage of coverages or [different] kind[s] of coverage," as Schramm's more recent work has found (1981: 214). That is to say, nonaligned nations do have available to their news media a number of alternatives to TNNA newswires. Unfortunately it seems that Third World papers remain in a position of heavy reliance upon the TNNAs for timely, up-to-the-minute coverage of most of the globe. Editors are in the unenviable position of relying on TNNA coverage, even though these findings show reports taken from the Big Four to be lacking in several respects that are of growing importance to both journalists and political leaders of developing nations (Roser and Brown, 1986).

Looking to the final question, the data clearly show that a vertical flow does characterize the structure of international communication. News flows today show a striking similarity to the imperial system of preferences that was created by the Ring Combination's cartel of a century ago. International news flows are neocolonial in at least two respects. First of all, three former British colonies get their largest percentage of international news (roughly one-third) from the British wire service. Similarly, four out of every ten foreign reports in the Latin American press are carried by the two American agencies combined. Therefore, information coming into these Third World nations follows a moderately neocolonial pattern. Secondly, in regard to information flowing out of LDCs, the evidence indicates interactions of an even more pronounced neoimperial nature. A strong relationship exists between a Third World nation's former colonial power and the Western wire service (or services) which gathers information within that LDC. Roughly 70 percent of the news from the U.S. sphere of influence, 50 percent of the news from the British domain, and 45 percent of news from areas formerly under French suzerainty has been directed to the developing presses studied here by the TNNAs of each respective power (see Figure 3.1).

Figure 3.1 presents a picture of the neocolonial structure of news flows. One can clearly see that the *framework* is essentially the same as the "feudal interaction patterns" described by Galtung. Periphery-to-Center and Center-to-Periphery vertical flows are evident within each imperial sphere. On the other hand, related studies to be presented in the following chapters will show that the *effects* of the system are not as structuralists have predicted. The neocolonial structure has been said to promote cultural im-

Figure 3.1:
The Neocolonial Structure of International News Flows

```
           US                    |          UK                   |        FRANCE
                                 |                               |
    ┌─────────────────┐          |    ┌─────────────────┐        |   ┌─────────────────┐
    │   Periphery     │          |    │   Periphery     │        |   │   Periphery     │
    └─────────────────┘          |    └─────────────────┘        |   └─────────────────┘
          │ - 70%                |          │ - 50%              |         │ - 45%
          ▼                      |          ▼                    |         ▼
    ┌─────────────────┐          |    ┌─────────────────┐        |   ┌─────────────────┐
    │     Center      │          |    │     Center      │        |   │     Center      │
    │   (AP + UPI)    │          |    │    (Reuters)    │        |   │     (AFP)       │
    └─────────────────┘          |    └─────────────────┘        |   └─────────────────┘
      │ 40%  │ 40%  │            |      │ 33% │ 33%  │           |     │  ?  │  ?  │
      ▼      ▼      ▼            |      ▼     ▼      ▼           |     ▼     ▼     ▼
     La     La    Excl.          |     D.    Zam.   Zbw.         |    * * * * * * * *
    Nacion  Prensa               |    Nation Times  Herld        |
                                 |                               |
   85% of all                    |   50-75% of all               |    ?  ?  ?  ?  ?
   international                 |   international               |
   news is "internal"            |   news is "internal"          |
   (RE this sphere).             |   (RE this sphere).           |
```

perialism and domestic instability in LDCs. Chapter Four will show Western media to be largely unrelated to cultural hegemony in the Third World. Furthermore, a free flow of media into and within the developing countries can be shown to be associated with political stability there rather than promoting domestic unrest (see Chapter Five).

NOTES

1. *Statistics on Radio and Television 1960–1976* (Paris: Unesco, 1978).
2. For my purposes, data are required on both total hours of broadcasting and hours of broadcasting imported. Data exist on both of these factors for radio and television for twenty-one nations: Algeria, Barbados, Brazil, Burundi, Cameroon, the Central African Republic, Cyprus, Ethiopia, Gambia, Ghana, Iran, Iraq, Jamaica, Jordan, South Korea, Mauritius, Nigeria, the Philippines, the Sudan, Trinidad and Tobago, and Tunisia. Additional data on total hours and hours imported for just radio were available for fourteen nations: Botswana, Guyana, Lebanon, Liberia, Malawi, Morocco, Nepal, Niger, Panama, Rwanda, Sri Lanka, Swaziland, Togo, and Western Somoa. Finally, I also added in data for eight nations for total/ imported hours of television broadcasting (only): Chile, India, Malaysia, Pakistan, Saudi Arabia, Senegal, Singapore, and Syria.

3. A best-case test is one that would most fairly and clearly evaluate the validity of a given claim on the basis of its own arguments. I want to conduct tests with results directly relevant to the claims made within Unesco in favor of the NWIO (see also the tests in Chapters Four and Five).

4. There are certain obvious constraints placed upon the generalizability of findings from this study, given the fact that no papers from Francophone Africa are included. I will not be able to speak directly to the conditions of print media in those nations, but results from this study will have direct implications regarding postcolonial communication in LDCs of all regions. See the section below on tests of the claim that interstate communications are neocolonial in structure.

5. Each paper was sampled from all available issues for the periods of December 1983 to May 1984, or from December 1984 to May 1985. Because of problems with access to African dailies during 1984, issues were available for the *Daily Nation* only for the months of December, January, February, March, and May. For the Zimbabwe *Herald*, issues were available for January through May. The *Times of Zambia* was available only for the months of April and May. No such problems existed for the samples drawn during 1985 from both the African and Latin American papers. Care was also taken so that no two issues of the same paper were taken from the same week.

6. This task was complicated somewhat by the fact that both the *Herald* and the *Times* report all of their stories by including their respective national news agencies in every byline. For the purposes of coding, I assumed that the majority of that portion of the report coming from overseas was carried via the TNNAs.

7. Cf. Note 6.

8. In those areas where colonial powers did not have formal colonies—but in which one imperial nation historically held sway in matters of military hegemony and/or international communication (e.g., the United Kingdom in Egypt)—stories from that region were coded according to the Western power which was dominant in the area.

4
International Communication and Cultural Imperialism

On 31 December, 1984, the United States withdrew its membership from the United Nations Educational, Scientific, and Cultural Organization (Unesco). The Reagan Administration cited as reasons for withdrawing the rapid growth in Unesco's budget, alleged mismanagement of Unesco programs, Soviet subversion of Unesco's policies (e.g., an "education for disarmament" campaign), and Unesco's support for programs that allegedly threaten freedom of the press. Problems with the budget and management have been acknowledged by Unesco's directors, and the organization has recently submitted to outside audits (Jacobson, 1984). The perceived threats to an international free press remain, however, and have contributed most to the Administration's decision to opt out of Unesco entirely. The consensus within the Administration and among many Western nations is that Unesco's campaign for a New World Information Order (NWIO), organized and pushed forward by a coalition of the Soviets and the Third World, represents an attempt to restrict the ability of the Western press to perform certain necessary political functions. The NWIO, they argue, would change the mass media from a watchdog on governmental abuse into a vehicle for official propaganda.

For their part, the Third World nations see the NWIO campaign as part of a larger effort to fundamentally restructure international relations. The NIEO (introduced in 1976), along with the New International Economic Order (NIEO) (introduced in 1974), is seen as a means to break out of what the Third World perceives to be a state of structural dependency.

This chapter appeared in *International Interactions* (1987), 13 (4), under the title "Testing Theories of Cultural Imperialism: International Media and Domestic Impact." It appears here by permission of Gordon and Breach Science Publishers.

Toward that end, many champions of the NWIO are much more concerned with ending Western domination of international communication flows than with protecting the freedom of the world's various press institutions.

In the view of many Third World nations, the most central point of contention in the NWIO debate regards the deleterious effects that international communication has upon the cultures of less developed countries (LDCs). Policy-oriented diplomats from LDCs and theorists of the structural school share a common thesis regarding Third World cultural development. Both groups charge that Western nations control flows of international news and information, allowing them to undermine the cultures of the rest of the world.[1] NWIO advocates at Unesco and structuralists in academic circles come back to this point time and time again when identifying the alleged pernicious effects that the extant system of international communication has on LDCs (Becker et al., 1986; Galtung, 1979; Masmoudi, 1981; McPhail, 1987; Schiller, 1976).

The structural thesis holds that Western media serve as a vehicle for Western values, Western norms, and Western culture. Along with news and entertainment, Western media carry to the LDCs images of a more prosperous life and more exciting lifestyles. To the extent that Third World nations are dependent upon the West for their international news and entertainment broadcasting, they allegedly become molded in the West's cultural image.

Pictures of the Western way of life are said to create social, political, and economic changes in the Third World through the demonstration effect. Western mass media allegedly stimulate desires on the part of the Third World to emulate Western culture (Cardoso and Faletto, 1979: 12–27). This is a way of life based largely on capitalist economies and consumer-oriented markets. As demands for a more westernized lifestyle increase, so do the demands for Western goods. This, in turn, allegedly leads to increased importation of Western commodities and increased dependence by LDCs on their Northern trading partners. According to Anthony Smith, "the flow of media exports [by the West] acts as a kind of ideological prerequisite for the flow of other material exports" (1980: 43). This is the condition of cultural imperialism, also referred to by Thomas McPhail as "electronic colonialism":

Electronic colonialism is the dependency relationship established by the importation of communication hardware, foreign-produced software, along with engineers, technicians, and related information protocols, that vicariously establish a set of foreign norms, values, and expectations which, in varying degrees, may alter the domestic cultures and socialization processes. (1987: 18)

McPhail goes on to say that electronic colonialism is stimulated by a wide range of Western products, including "[c]omic books to satellites, computers to lasers, along with more traditional fare such as radio programs, theater, movies, and wire services to television shows" (*ibid.*).

To assess the argument that links inputs of Western media fare to cultural changes in developing nations, the thesis of cultural imperialism must be specified, operationalized, and tested empirically. This can be done by constructing a faithful, best-case series of tests to give structural arguments an equitable evaluation.[2] Once the results from this series of empirical tests have been presented, their implications for structural theories of cultural imperialism will become evident.

THE STRUCTURAL THESIS OF CULTURAL IMPERIALISM

The most theoretically sophisticated treatment of the alleged structural links between international communication and cultural imperialism can be found in the work of Johan Galtung. Galtung's three phases in the history of imperialism are distinguished primarily by their distinct technologies of communication (and transportation). According to Galtung, the global development of imperialism is a function of the means by which the Western powers have established a "harmony of interests" between themselves and the dependent economies of the South. In the third and emerging stage of imperialism, this means is the "instant communication" afforded by telesatellites and the movement of (or access to) enormous computer data banks across national boundaries. Such instant communication allegedly facilitates control of the North over the South even more effectively than the old means of military occupation or economic domination by multinational corporations (1979: 167).

In addition to his historical argument, which bases the development of imperialism on communication technologies, Galtung identifies five types of imperialism: economic, political, military, communication, and cultural. Given his historical argument, one would expect the impact of communication imperialism to be increasing rapidly in Galtung's view. This is the case. In fact, although Galtung says that imperialism can be introduced in any one of these five forms and then spread to the others, it is in communication imperialism that Galtung finds the primary impetus to cultural imperialism (1979: 164–166).

For Galtung and other structuralists (Harris, 1981b: 358) the international system of communication is characterized by a "feudal interaction structure." Communication within this structure is said to be almost entirely vertical (from the West to the LDCs, or vice versa) with little or no horizontal communication taking place (between the LDCs themselves) due to two fundamental reasons. First, the high levels of industrial capacity and technological innovation required to develop new generations of communication hardware exist only in the developed economies of North America, western Europe, and Japan. Communication satellites would be one recent example. Second, the Western news agencies which dominate international news gathering and dissemination are themselves "feudal" in structure. According to structural thought, the four Western international news agencies (AFP, AP, Reuters, and UPI) are controlled by Western business elites who see to it that the focus of international reporting is on those events and issues most important to their own interests. News about the West takes up a much larger proportion of the Third World press than vice versa. Events in all parts of the globe, including the Third World, are said to be seen by LDCs through Western eyes. LDCs produce events, usually of a crisis nature, that the Western press define only in terms of their significance to Western interests. These conditions, ones that characterize communication imperialism, bring "us straight into cultural imperialism" according to Galtung (1979: 166). That is, for the structuralists, cultural imperialism is largely a product of communication imperialism.

Galtung cites news exchanges between the North and the South as a "combination of cultural and communication exchanges." In a process by which the West inundates LDCs with news and information originating in the more developed nations, the West "always provides the teachers"—teachers of the road to economic and political development, teachers of a new and supposedly better culture—and the Third World "always provides the learners." This, according to Galtung, is "a pattern which smacks of imperialism." At this point Galtung also argues that there is an important structural link between Western sources of information and educational processes within LDCs. Galtung concludes his discussion on the five types of imperialism by pointing to a "brain drain"—a process allegedly stimulated and maintained by Western control of international communication and a process that saps the LDCs of their most important intellectual resource, students, for the benefit of the West.[3] Galtung also argues that finished intellectual products (academic journals, books, educational curricula) are sent by the West to LDCs only "after first having created a demand for [them] through the demonstration effect" (1979: 166).

The structural thesis of cultural imperialism holds that Western mass media and other sources of information create a demonstration effect in LDCs which, in time, undermines or destroys the indigenous values and cultures of these latter states. If this thesis is correct, one would expect to find that those LDCs which import more Western media are also those which tend to become most like the West culturally. High levels of Western media imports would have to be closely associated with a strong tendency to adopt Western cultural traits.

INITIAL SPECIFICATION OF THE THESIS OF CULTURAL IMPERIALISM

Figure 4.1 (below) contains two hypotheses which represent initial specifications of the structural thesis of cultural imperialism. H1 states that

Figure 4.1:
Initial Specification of the Structural Thesis

	DEPENDENT VARIABLE	INDEPENDENT VARIABLE(S)
H1	Cultural Imperialism	= f(Media Dependency)
H2	Westernization	= f(Media Imports, Press Freedom)

cultural imperialism in Third World nations is a function of media dependency by these nations on the West. H2 puts the same argument into slightly more specific terms. It states that westernization is a function of imported (Western) media content and levels of press freedom in the Third World. NWIO advocates have argued that free-press institutions are inappropriate to the needs and limits of political development of LDCs. In the following sections, this thesis will be further specified, operationalized, and then tested.

The empirical research presented here was designed to produce evidence that must either support or deny the theoretical claims of Galtung, Harris, Schiller, and others. Once the results of the quantitative tests are presented, the findings will be analyzed, giving special attention to their implications for the structuralists' arguments.

Specifically, the focus in the remainder of this chapter will be on three areas:

1. The relationship between media policies and media imports in the Third World (on the one hand), and the adoption of Western economic models by Third World nations.
2. The relationship between media policies/imports, and a draining of students away from the Third World.
3. The relationship between media policies/imports and the adoption of Western lifestyles in the Third World (based on the importation of consumer goods and Western-style luxuries).

FURTHER SPECIFICATION OF THE STRUCTURAL THESIS

Testing for cultural imperialism requires establishing whether LDCs that import more information from Western sources are also the developing nations that tend to have more westernized socio-economic systems. To investigate adequately the relevant aspects of this argument requires a series of tests. The measures of cultural homogeneity (the process of be-

Figure 4.2:
Further Specification of the Structural Thesis

DEPENDENT VARIABLE	INDEPENDENT VARIABLES
H3a Economic System	= f(Media Imports, Press Freedom)
H3b Educational System	= f(Media Imports, Press Freedom)
H3c Consumption	= f(Media Imports, Press Freedom)

coming more like the West culturally) in this chapter will be based on a number of different items: a) business practices; b) educational trends; and c) particular imported goods, or distribution of imports according to broad types. These are alternative means of measuring important social and economic traits that would be similar to those in the West.

The hypotheses in Figure 4.1 are based on structural literature as it now stands. Such hypotheses, however, are still too diffuse to allow for rigorous empirical testing. Figure 4.2 contains three further hypotheses that can be extrapolated from the claims put forth by the structuralists. Each is a further specification of H2 in a particular social or economic realm. H3a through H3c are suggested by the claims made in the structural literature, but none is explicitly stated in that body of work.

H3a states that an LDC's economic system (e.g., economic structure and business practices) is a function of foreign media and press freedom. H3b states that Third World educational systems (e.g., curricula, place of education) are a function of press freedom and imported media. H3c states that patterns of consumption in LDCs (e.g., sources and types of consumer goods) are a function of press freedom and media imports.

H3a is suggested by the work of Schiller (1981; 1976). H3b is suggested in both Galtung's (1980) and Schiller's work. H3c is suggested by the claims made by many structuralists and *dependencia* theorists (Cardoso and Faletto, 1979; Galtung, 1979; Masmoudi, 1981; McPhail, 1987; Harris, 1981b).

The subsequent discussion will explain how the concepts in hypotheses H3a, H3b, and H3c are to be operationalized. Methods of sampling and the rationale behind each series of tests will also be explained. One general point should be made. Each hypothesis in Figure 4.2 will first be operationalized in a simple and straightforward way. If such straightforward specifications of these hypotheses do not yield evidence to support structural claims, however, the tests will not necessarily end at that point. In order to give structural arguments a truely fair test and in order to find a best-case test, additional trials may become necessary. These additional tests may be required to consider the possibilities of, for example, nonlinear relationships between variables, controlling for exogenous variables, interactions among variables, and tests on subsets of the original sample.

THE RESEARCH DESIGN

Operationalization of the Variables

The Independent Variables. The determining (independent) variables of the structural thesis allow for rather straightforward measurement. The extent to which a Third World nation imports broadcast media from the West can be easily determined by breaking down data from Unesco according to percentages of total broadcasting which are produced within the nation and those which are not.[4] Because the nations that export broadcast media on a global scale are almost exclusively Western countries, it is safe to assume that most of the media imported into the Third World comes from Western sources. According to the views of the structuralists, this constitutes another example of communication imperialism.

Measures on imported broadcasting, however, are not sufficient by themselves to gauge the extent of Western media circulation in Third World nations. One also needs to know how widely available these media are to Third World populations. If the governments of these states place tight restrictions on media programming, much of the imported media may not be accessible for large portions of the country. If Western media are not seen by the masses or, for that matter, by large portions of the elite, then there is little chance that the demonstration effect could have as large an impact on these nations as structuralists postulate.

In addition to broadcast media imports, a measure of press freedom in each state is therefore also required.[5] This will enable taking into account the extent to which foreign media may be widely distributed within these LDCs. A higher level of press freedom would tend to indicate that imported media of all kinds are more readily accessible for the inhabitants of these states. Those nations that wish to break out of their dependency on the West, according to structural theorists and NWIO advocates, need to employ stronger governmental controls on their national media. Adding a measure of press freedom will also allow for a check to see if this is sound advice. Do nations that employ tighter controls over media policies also tend to be those nations which have been more successful in combating cultural imperialism? The subsequent tests of the structural thesis will produce empirical evidence directly related to such questions.

Dependent Variable A: Westernization of the Economy. According to the structural thesis, the above are the independent variables. The dependent variable is the extent to which Third World cultures become homogenized in the Western model. To test this hypothesis requires measures that reflect economic and social systems characteristic of the West. The indicators must be ones which clearly separate the West from other socioeconomic systems (e.g., the Soviet model) that Third World nations might pattern themselves after in their drive for modernization. A signal characteristic of the Western productive system, and a trait which differentiates it clearly from most of its Eastern bloc rivals, is the heavy emphasis it places on a consumer-oriented economy (Gilpin, 1981: 83). Third World nations that follow the West's lead will attempt to achieve growth by stimulating increased consumption and consumer demand. Instead of employing highly centralized and highly planned forms of production, they will tend to rely more heavily on free markets and consumer demand to determine which sectors of the economy will grow most rapidly (see Frenkle and O'Donnell, 1979; Friedman, 1973: 59–61). Western analysts and financial institutions dominated by the West (such as the International Monetary Fund) will normally recommend reliance upon market forces, comparative advantage, and private enterprise to pursue growth within the context and constraints of extant international trading regimes (Krasner, 1985).

If a consumer-oriented economy is a good indicator of a Western approach to national development, what is a good indicator of consumer economies? Advertising helps to keep Western consumer economies functioning. Large advertising expenditures aid Western economic expansion by stimulating demand, thereby increasing industrial output. The same would be true of Third World nations if they became infected with the "disease" of cultural imperialism. Those LDCs with larger yearly advertising expenditures will also tend to be the developing nations that rely most on relatively free markets to stimulate growth and determine production levels. On the other hand, Third World nations with centralized planning as their means for national development see little value in large advertising expenditures. Advertising in those states is generally viewed as a costly waste of severely limited resources.

For their part, structuralists have also identified consumer economies and concomitantly large advertising expenditures as signs of Western cultural hegemony. It is in this respect that McPhail has said: "Western advertising [is] seen as a threat in the Third World" (1987: 21). Advertising is seen as a threat because it often reflects the adoption of Western values and Western styles of business (Roser and Brown, 1986: 118). Advertising is also a threat, in the structuralist's view, because it allegedly increases a dependency on the West by increasing the demand for luxuries and consumer goods exported by the West.

Herbert Schiller, noted structuralist, recommends self-sufficiency in communication technologies, centralized planning, and protectionist media policies to Third World nations as a means for breaking out of their structural dependency. Schiller's ultimate aims are not just to decrease the importation of Western media into LDCs. Self-sufficiency and protectionism are policies designed to go beyond mere media reform. They are proposals that Schiller believes will also create fundamental changes in the economic systems of LDCs. They will help to do away with Western styles of advertising and consumer-oriented economies in a drive to establish new controls over consumption patterns. Only after certain preliminary steps have been taken in the realm of communication reform will it be possible for LDCs to turn their economic capacities away from "luxuries"—items for which a demand is allegedly stimulated via imported media and the demonstration effect—and toward production to fill "basic human needs" (1967: 61). Attacks on imported media and press freedom are Schiller's means for destroying consumer economies and the consumption of luxuries, thus reflecting his belief in the existence of causal links between these processes.

A good indicator of a Western-style economic system is one that can identify those nations which rely on consumer-oriented economies; economies which are based in part on large advertising outlays. The first measure of westernization of the Third World in the economic realm, then, will be yearly advertising expenditures. But it is also necessary to take into account the size of a nation's population (advertising relative to national size). Therefore, yearly advertising per capita is a reasonable indicator of westernized economies in the Third World.[6]

Dependent Variable B: Westernization of the Educational System. Of course, advertising is not the only important similarity between a Western culture and those cultures of the Third World that may have been subjected to cultural hegemony. Galtung and others (Schiller, 1976: 11) have pointed to particular types of educational curricula and an alleged brain drain (more properly referred to as a student drain) in the Third World as indicators of cultural imperialism. This allows for another way to test the structural thesis: retaining the determining variables of press freedom and media imports, but substituting levels of Third World students who are educated in the West for advertising (as the dependent variable).[7] The measure of Western cultural hegemony in a developing nation would then be the extent to which their students are sent to Western centers of higher education. According to the structural thesis, one would expect those Third World nations with higher levels of press freedom and imported media (hence subject to cultural imperialism) to also tend to be nations which lose more of their best students to Western educational institutions.

Dependent Variable C: Westernization of Consumption. A third general approach to testing the structural thesis would be to look at cultural imperialism in terms of the lifestyles found in the Third World—rather than in terms of business and educational trends. Studying the ways that people of developing nations live, as reflected in their consumption patterns, may

Figure 4.3:
Third Specification of the Cultural Imperialism Thesis

H3a/Equation [4.1] $ADV = a + B_1 MI + B_2 PF + e$

H3b/Equation [4.2] $EDUC = a + B_1 MI + B_2 PF + e$

H3c/Equation [4.3] $LUX = a + B_1 MI + B_2 PF + e$

ADV = advertising per capita
       (source: Starch, INRA, Hooper, 1982)
EDUC = students educated in the West
       (source: Unesco, 1981)
LUX = expenditures on imported luxuries
       (source: United Nations, 1982)
MI   = percentage of broadcast media imported
       (source: Unesco, 1978)
PF   = score on press freedom scale
       (source: Kurian, 1979)
a   = constant (intercept)
e   = error term

---

be a better way to judge whether these nations have become westernized. We have already discussed Schiller's condemnation of certain luxury items as products of westernization which are inappropriate to the needs of LDCs with severely limited resources. Items such as color televisions, private automobiles, yachts, and expensive cosmetics and jewelry reflect what Schiller sees as a decadent Western lifestyle. This is a lifestyle allegedly imported into the Third World as a product of foreign media and the demonstration effect. If this argument of the structuralists is sound, then those Third World nations with greater press freedom and larger proportions of imported media will also tend to be those nations which spend more on such luxuries. A third measure of cultural homogeneity, then, would be the levels of such goods imported into each Third World nation.[8]

Based on operationalizing the variables in these modes, Hypotheses H3a, H3b, and H3c can be specified in terms of the equations in Figure 4.3.

Each of the three equations in Figure 4.3 states that westernization is a function of a linear, additive relationship with imported media and press freedom. Equation [4.1] operationalizes westernization of the economic system as yearly advertising per capita. Equation [4.2] operationalizes westernization of the educational system as numbers of students from each Third World nation who are educated in the West. Equation [4.3] operationalizes westernization of lifestyles as luxury goods imported into LDCs.[9]

The Sample

Nations that fall under the heading "Third World" are extremely diverse. They differ widely in their political ideologies, cultures, and levels of economic development. Any sample that hopes to be at all representative of the Third World as a whole must take these facts into consideration. The sample used in most of the following tests consists of twenty-four nations that reflect the diversity of the Third World in several important respects. Nations in the sample were Argentina, Brazil, Chile, Colombia, Egypt, Ethiopia, Ghana, India, Iran, Iraq, Jamaica, Jordan, Lebanon, Mexico, Morocco, Nigeria, Pakistan, Panama, Singapore, South Korea, Sri Lanka, Syria, Uruguay, and Zambia.

This sample population is large enough to contain roughly one out of every five LDCs. Included are nations from Latin America, Africa, the Middle East, and Asia. The sample includes nations with a wealth of oil reserves and nations that are relatively well developed economically (compared with the rest of the Third World). The sample also includes many nations that are among the poorest in the Third World (such as those in sub-Saharan Africa). This particular sample was drawn to meet two integrated criteria. First, it incorporates the most current data available on as many developing nations as possible, making the sample as large as possible. Second, it reflects a wide range in levels of economic development, cultural backgrounds, and political systems. Furthermore, problems with availability of data (or lack of it) preclude the use of a simple random sample taken from the population of all Third World nations.

Aggregate data on advertising, students educated in the West, and other economic variables were gathered for each of these nations. These data are the most recent available, representing conditions in those nations during the middle and late 1970s. However, conclusions drawn from these data are also relevant to an understanding of international communication and the political economies of Third World nations in the 1980s. This is true due to the context in which the Third World must pursue development. The elements of the international system of communication discussed previously characterized the decades of the seventies and eighties and, in all probability, will hold true for the foreseeable future. Advantages in resources and technology enjoyed by Western nations put them in the favored position in international communication. The communications technologies and newswires of the West are, by far, the most advanced and far-reaching. The same basic contraints which applied to Third World development and communication industries in the past will also tend to remain for the foreseeable future. Barring some drastic restructuring of the international sys-

Table 4.1:
Coefficients for Equation [4.1]

VARIABLE	UNSTANDARDIZED COEFFICIENT	STANDARDIZED COEFFICIENT	t-RATIO
MI	.066	.18	.93
PF	2.41	.41	2.12*

Dependent Variable = ADV   intercept = 4.63
R^2 = .23   adjusted R^2 = .15   N = 24   s.e. = 8.10

ADV = advertising per capita
 (source: Starch, INRA, Hooper, 1982)
MI = media imported (source: Unesco, 1978)
PF = press freedom ranking on an 8-point scale
 (source: Kurian, 1979)

* = statistically significant, .05 level; two-tailed test

tems of economics and information (which is highly unlikely, given the breakdown of negotiations on the NIEO and NWIO) the same broad context will remain in the Third World for many years to come.[10]

FIRST TEST OF THE STRUCTURAL THESIS

The first test of the structural thesis is based on Equation [4.1]. This equation conceptualizes westernization in terms of advertising expenditures, and media dependency in terms of imports plus press freedom. Equation [4.1] states that a Third World nation's level of yearly advertising per capita is a function of the amount of media it imports from the West as well as the extent to which it pursues a national policy of a free press. When the structural thesis is stated in these terms and the variables are operationalized, the empirical results are as shown in Table 4.1.

The unstandardized estimate for PF shows that an increase of one full unit on the eight-unit press freedom scale is associated (on the average) with a $2.41 increase in yearly advertising per capita (independent of the effects of imported media). The estimate for MI can be interpreted as revealing that an increase of 20 percent in the proportion of total broadcasting which is imported (say from 10 percent to 30 percent) will be associated with, on average, an increase of $1.32 in yearly advertising per capita (while controlling for press freedom). The slope intercept (4.63) can be interpreted to mean that a nation which has a rating of zero on the press freedom index, and which also imports no broadcast media whatsoever, would (on the average) spend $4.63 per capita per year on advertising.[11] Unfortunately this equation provides only a mildly adequate fit

Table 4.2:
Coefficients for Equation [4.1a]

VARIABLE	UNSTANDARDIZED COEFFICIENT	STANDARDIZED COEFFICIENT	t-RATIO
MI	.053	.15	.70
PF	2.35	.40	2.03
GNP	.0002	.11	.52

Dependent Variable = ADV   intercept = 4.54
R^2 = .24   adjusted R^2 = .12   N = 24   s.e. = 8.25

GNP = per capita Gross National Product
 (source: Unesco, 1978; and Starch, INRA, Hooper, 1982)
other sources: see Table 4.1

---

for the data on foreign media inputs and westernization in the Third World. Only 23 percent of the variance in advertising per capita can be accounted for in terms of the variance in press freedom and media imports combined.

Of course, there may be other processes which help to determine yearly advertising expenditures in Third World nations. These could be processes which act independently of national policies regarding press freedom and imported media. An obvious example of such a factor would be the nation's level of economic development. More highly developed Third World states may tend to spend more on advertising, regardless of their media policies, merely because they have more economic resources with which to work. To control for this possibility, Hypothesis H3a can be restated in terms of Equation [4.1a]:

H3a/Equation [4.1a] $ADV = a + B_1 MI + B_2 PF + B_3 GNP + e$

Controlling for Gross National Product (GNP)[12] assures that variance in advertising, which is closely associated with variance in economic prosperity is not reflected spuriously in the parameter estimates for media imports and press freedom. Stated in these terms, the results of this test of the structural thesis are as shown in Table 4.2.

All common elements in Equations [4.1] and [4.1a] have the same meaning. The new element in Equation [4.1a], GNP, is a measure of GNP per capita. Controlling for GNP per capita has had a noticable (but slight) effect on the estimates for press freedom and imported media. On the basis of Equation [4.1a] one would say that a one-unit increase on the press freedom index is associated with an increase of $2.35 in yearly advertising per capita (on the average, while holding media imports and level of development constant). A check of the standardized coefficients shows that press freedom is also the most important variable in this equation in terms of its ability to account for variance in advertising expenditures.[13] According to Equation [4.1a], an additional 20 percent of all broadcasting coming from foreign sources would be associated with an increase of $1.06 (on average, independent of PF and GNP). Surprisingly, an increase in GNP per capita of $1,000 is associated with only a 20-cent increase in advertising per capita (on average, holding press freedom and media imports constant). Controlling for levels of economic development yields only a slightly better fit for the equation to the data (the R^2 increases from .23 to only .24, while the adjusted R^2 actually decreases). None of the parameter estimates in this equation are significant either.

These first two equations assume that the determining variables in the model (press freedom, media imports, GNP per capita) act independently of one another. This assumption was made to keep these first tests relatively simple and straightforward. This assumption, however, could be a faulty one. It is possible that two or more variables interact with each other in addition to affecting advertising expenditures. There are even some theoretical considerations that imply that this may be the case.

Classic democratic theory has long held that as nations develop economically they also tend to become increasingly pluralized in their politics. More economic wealth is said to lead to new and more numerous political groups in society with their "crosscutting cleavages" (for treatments which apply this position to politics in developing nations see Apter, 1965; Lerner, 1958).

In much the same way, one might expect that increased economic development also leads to a more pluralized media. As a nation becomes more developed, according to this argument, more media outlets (e.g., publications, broadcasting stations) become economically viable. More views and more varied views can then be expressed through the media. New elites form with positions on various issues, elites which seek media outlets to see that their views are heard.

If this argument were correct, one would expect the number of national media outlets to interact with levels of press freedom in their impact on advertising. That is, as more media outlets become available, they may or may not lead to an increase in the dissemination of Western media content, depending on the levels of press freedom which obtain in each state. According to structuralist thinking, if an LDC has many media outlets and a high level of press freedom, then it is in the situation which is most vulnerable to cultural hegemony. On the other hand, a nation with many media outlets but less press freedom is (according to this logic) in less danger of succumbing to the forces of cultural imperialism because the demonstration effect can be diverted through controls on media content. A similar logic could also be spun out for nations with few media outlets and different levels of press freedom.

Table 4.3:
Coefficients for Equation [4.1b]

VARIABLE	UNSTANDARDIZED COEFFICIENT	STANDARDIZED COEFFICIENT	t-RATIO
PF x GNP	.0005	.31	1.46
MI	.055	.15	.72

Dependent Variable = ADV   intercept = 5.18
R^2 = .15   adjusted R^2 = .07   N = 24   s.e. = 8.51

sources: see Tables 4.1 and 4.2

To test for the possibility that this argument is correct, one would need a measure which specifies the interaction of press freedom with the number of media outlets in a nation. No data are available for the total number of media outlets in the Third World. However, recall that the notion of media outlets became important because it was argued to be closely related to economic development. It may be reasonable to argue that economic development produces a pluralized media, in much the same way that others have argued economic development leads to pluralized politics. Although no useful data exist on total media outlets, because the assumption is that increased development is strongly correlated with more media outlets, another indicator of development can be substituted for the estimate of total media outlets. The measure of development in Equation 4.1a, GNP per capita, should serve nicely for this purpose. An interactive term (press freedom times GNP per capita) was constructed and entered into Equation [4.1b], and the parameters were reestimated (see Table 4.3):

H3a/Equation [4.1b] $ADV = a + B_1 MI + B_2 (PF \times GNP) + e$

The new factor in Equation [4.1b] is the interactive variable. The estimate for media imports (MI) remains virtually unchanged from the previous equation. There is also no intuitive interpretation for PF × GNP. Postulating an interaction between press freedom and development gives this test a less desirable fit to the empirical data. The multiple coefficient of determination has dropped from .24 to .15, indicating that a theory which argues that there is an interaction between press freedom and development has less empirical support than one which maintains that these two factors operate largely independent of each another. This equation is also less adequate than Equation [4.1] because none of the partial slope estimates are statistically significant.

An additional consideration should be taken into account at this point. These first three equations all assume the relationships between the dependent and independent variables to be intrinsically linear. Again, this was a simplifying assumption made to keep the first tests relatively straightforward. Linear regression assumes that levels of ADV (advertising) change at roughly the same rate for increases across the entire ranges of all the independent variables (press freedom, media imports, GNP per capita). A check of the bivariate scatterplots, however, suggests that this assumption does not hold for one of the determining variables. Levels of advertising increase at a slow, gradual rate for ascending levels of press freedom below zero. Above this point on the scale, however, advertising per capita increases at a rapid (almost exponential) rate. It would appear that increases in press freedom within the negative half of the scale are associated with much smaller increases in advertising than are increases at the positive end of the scale.[14]

A curvilinear relationship between advertising and press freedom makes sense if we stop to ponder the considerations on which a business bases its advertising decisions. Funds spent on advertising would tend to produce a much better return (the effect of advertising in stimulating business will be greater) at higher levels of press freedom. At higher levels, less restrictive governmental media policies will allow for greater numbers of people to be reached by a given advertisement. This means that investments of advertising dollars will tend to have a greater impact (and hence a higher return) at higher levels of press freedom. Therefore, once press freedom passes a certain point, more businesses will tend to invest more of their resources in advertising. Added competition from their business rivals would also tend to induce all firms to turn more toward advertising to attract their customers. To incorporate this nonlinear relationship into the test, a logarithmic transformation of the dependent variable is required (Tufte, 1974; see also Sartwell and Anello cited in Tufte at p. 126). After performing this transformation the semilog model can be estimated as stated in Equation [4.1c]:

H3a/Equation [4.1c] $LOGADV = a + B_1MI + B_2PF + B_3GNP + e$

LOGADV represents the common logarithm of advertising per capita. As one can see from Table 4.4 (below), this model provides the best fit yet to the empirical data. A relatively strong fit is evident in the fact that a full 41 percent of the variance of the common log of advertising per capita is associated with the combined variance of press freedom, media imports, and GNP per capita. The semilog model also provides an interesting additional interpretation for the parameter estimates. Using Tufte's method of solving by taking antilogarithms (1974: 127–128), one could say that a one-unit increase in press freedom is associated with a 70 percent increase in advertising per capita (on the average, controlling for MI and GNP). An increase in imported broadcasting (as a proportion of total

Table 4.4:
Coefficients for Equation [4.1c]

VARIABLE	UNSTANDARDIZED COEFFICIENT	STANDARDIZED COEFFICIENT	t-RATIO
MI	.005	.19	1.00
PF	.23	.53	3.02*
GNP	.00002	.14	.78

Dependent Variable = LOGADV intercept = .25
R^2 = .41   adjusted R^2 = .32   N = 24   s.e. = .55

sources: see Tables 4.1 and 4.2

* = significant at .05

broadcasting) of 20 percent is associated with, on average, a 24 percent increase in advertising per capita (holding the other independent variables constant). Unfortunately the estimate for a one-unit increase in GNP per capita is so small that it cannot be interpreted adequately through this method.[15]

Testing for Cultural Imperialism in the Fourth World

Before turning to tests of Hypotheses H3b and H3c, one further consideration should be taken into account regarding H3a. Up to this point, the discussion has been focused on the relationships between communication, westernization, and development in the Third World as a whole. The nations which fall under this rubric represent a great range of diversity. Not only do they differ from the West markedly, but they also differ from one another culturally, ideologically, and in levels of economic development. As was pointed out, the sample of twenty-four nations was drawn with these considerations in mind.

But what of different subgroups of nations within the Third World? Katz and Wedell (1977) have shown that different colonial and post-independence experiences can be very important in determining the institutional structures of broadcast media in the Third World. The authors found that one of the crucial factors in setting particular media policies in LDCs was whether a given nation was formerly a colony of France or of the United Kingdom. This might lead one to inquire about other explanatory categories into which Third World nations could be divided in order to give us a better understanding of the effects of communication and westernization in those parts of the world.

Some of the coefficients in the first four tests may strike students of the

Table 4.5:
Coefficients for Equation [4.1a]: Fourth World

VARIABLE	UNSTANDARDIZED COEFFICIENT	STANDARDIZED COEFFICIENT	t-RATIO
MI	-.0018	-.01	.04
PF	.57	.18	.93
GNP	.0057	.66	3.43*

Dependent Variable = ADV intercept = -.50
R^2 = .59   adjusted R^2 = .51   N = 19   s.e. = 3.41

sources: see Tables 4.1 and 4.2

* = significant at .05

developing world as counterintuitive. This is especially true of the fact that press freedom was found to be much more important than increases in per capita GNP in accounting for business practices (e.g., advertising) employed in the Third World. Recall that no significant relationship was found between increased development (measured as GNP per capita) and the measure of westernization. Given these results, and keeping in mind Katz and Wedell's work, the testing of H3a can be pursued further by excluding the richest Third World nations from the sample. By dropping the five nations which rank highest in terms of GNP per capita, a sample remains which represents the poorest nations of the Third World.[16] These are nations which are often included in what is referred to as the "Fourth World."

This sample of Fourth World nations contains only those which have per capita GNPs of less than $2,000. With the nineteen nations which are left from the original sample, two of the most interesting equations were reestimated.[17] The parameter estimates for the reformulations of Equations [4.1a] and [4.1c] (for the sample of nineteen nations) are presented in Tables 4.5 and 4.6.

Looking at the Fourth World alone (see Table 4.5), there is a significant relationship between advertising per capita (the measure of economic westernization) and GNP per capita (the measure of economic development). Furthermore, press freedom is no longer statistically significant in accounting for variance in the dependent variable. Comparing Equation [4.1a] for the Third World to Equation [4.1a] for the Fourth World, one finds that in the Fourth World an increase in GNP per capita of $1,000 is associated with an average increase in advertising per capita of $5.70 (instead of $.20), independent of the other explanatory variables. Looking at the Fourth World alone also gives these equations a much better fit to the empirical data, as the multiple coefficients of determination are much stronger. In

Table 4.6:
Coefficients for Equation [4.1c]: Fourth World

VARIABLES	UNSTANDARDIZED COEFFICIENT	STANDARDIZED COEFFICIENT	t-RATIO
MI	.0043	.13	1.00
PF	.08	.18	1.14
GNP	.0009	.72	4.69*

Dependent Variable = LOGADV   intercept = -.57
R^2 = .74   adjusted R^2 = .67   N = 19   s.e. = .37

sources: see Tables 4.1 and 4.2

---

* = significant at .05

the Fourth World, nearly 60 percent of the variance in advertising can be accounted for by variance in GNP per capita, press freedom, and media imports combined. This figure rises to 74 percent once advertising per capita is logged to account for its curvilinear relationship to the independent variables (see Table 4.6).

Before evaluating the implications of this first set of tests for the structural thesis of cultural imperialism, the discussion will turn to two other ways of testing the structural thesis. Tests up to this point have conceptualized cultural imperialism in terms of similarities between Western and Third World economic systems. So far the results have been mixed, finding press freedom to be most clearly related to consumer economies in the Third World as a whole and per capita GNP more relevant than press freedom in the Fourth World. In order to give structural arguments a fair test, what they have said about cultural hegemony in other areas must not be neglected. In the second and third tests of the structural argument, westernization will be conceptualized as changes in educational systems and changes in lifestyles, respectively.

SECOND TEST OF THE STRUCTURAL THESIS

Hypothesis H3b (see Figure 4.3) defines westernization of the Third World in terms of education. This hypothesis is based on the claims of Galtung and Schiller regarding the alleged student drain from the Third World to the West. Equation [4.2] has been slightly recast in the first test of H3b to prevent the estimates for PF and MI from spuriously picking up variance in EDUC which should be properly associated with differences in levels of economic development (i.e., GNP):

Table 4.7:
Coefficients for Equation [4.2a]

VARIABLE	UNSTANDARDIZED COEFFICIENT	STANDARDIZED COEFFICIENT	t-RATIO
MI	-50.0	-.20	.79
PF	581.0	.15	.60
GNP	-.75	-.11	.41

Dependent Variable = EDUC intercept = 8456
R^2 = .07   adjusted R^2 = -.04   N = 24   s.e. = 6242

EDUC = students educated in the West (source: Unesco, 1981)
other sources: see Tables 4.1 and 4.2

H3b/Equation [4.2a]   EDUC = a + B_1MI + B_2PF + B_3GNP + e

EDUC represents the number of students from Third World nations who are educated in the West. There is very little evidence from this test which could support the structural thesis. It would appear that an increase in press freedom of one unit would be associated with an average increase of 581 students educated in the West (see Table 4.7). However, on the basis of this sample of nations, one would say that increases in imported media from the West are actually associated with *decreases* in the number of students sent to the West for college educations. An increase of 1 percent in media imports is associated with an average decrease of fifty students educated in the West.

Increases in GNP per capita are also, perhaps less surprisingly, associated with average decreases in students sent abroad. A $100 rise in GNP per capita in this sample of nations is associated with an average decrease of seventy-five students sent to the West. This relationship can be explained, in part, by the fact that the more developed Third World nations (especially oil-rich sheikdoms) are building and improving their own universities in an effort to keep their young people at home. The inverse relationship between imported media and students is also consistent with prior research which has found something like a "reverse-demonstration" effect to be at work in some parts of the Third World, transmitting negative images of the far-from-perfect Western way of life, which may actually tend to persuade some students not to travel Westward for their education. A prior study (Hornik, 1975) found that young people living in rural Third World areas who have had more exposure to mass media are actually less likely to move to urban areas (see also Katz and Wedell, 1977: 181). But due to

Table 4.8:
Coefficients for Equation [4.2a]: Fourth World

VARIABLES	UNSTANDARDIZED COEFFICIENT	STANDARDIZED COEFFICIENT	t-RATIO
MI	-73.0	-.24	.91
PF	826.0	.20	.66
GNP	-1.0	-.09	.30

Dependent Variable = EDUC   intercept = 9197
R^2 = .07   adjusted R^2 = -.12   N = 19   s.e. = 6892

sources: see Tables 4.1, 4.2, and 4.7

---

the poor fit which this model provides for the data, such interpretations based on these parameters are risky at best. Also, because none of the estimates are statistically significant, few safe predictions can be made about Third World nations in general based on this sample.

Turning to the Fourth World again, Equation [4.2a] can be estimated, using the subsample of nineteen poorest nations. The parameter estimates then load as shown in Table 4.8.

Comparing the results of Equation [4.2a] for the larger and smaller samples shows that there is no clear (significant) relationship between increased economic development and students educated abroad, either in the Third World as a whole or in the Fourth World in particular. The tests do show, however, that there is a negative correlation between these phenomena within both samples.

THIRD AND FINAL TEST OF THE STRUCTURAL THESIS

The final test of structural claims is based on Hypothesis H3c. This test conceptualizes westernization of developing nations in terms of their lifestyles. Equation [4.3a] states H3c in terms of total expenditures for certain imported luxury items while, again, controlling for economic development. Equation [4.3b] states H3c in slightly different terms. In the second of these equations, imported Western items are expressed as the percentage of all imports which is devoted to consumer goods. Instead of adding independent variables as in some of the previous equations, the dependent variable changes from Equation [4.3a] to Equation [4.3b], but the general area of the test remains the same (lifestyle or consumption trends).

Table 4.9:
Coefficients for Equation [4.3a]

VARIABLE	UNSTANDARDIZED COEFFICIENT	STANDARDIZED COEFFICIENT	t-RATIO
MI	3321.0	.42	1.18
PF	128908.0	.69	2.05
GNP	-11.0	-.37	1.02

Dependent Variable = LUX   intercept = 155,406
R^2 = .48   adjusted R^2 = .17   N = 9   s.e. = 187,188

LUX = US dollars spent on selected imported luxury items (source: United Nations, 1982)
other sources: see Tables 4.1 and 4.2

H3c/Equation [4.3a] $LUX = a + B_1 MI + B_2 PF + B_3 GNP + e$

H3c/Equation [4.3b] $CONS = a + B_1 MI + B_2 PF + B_3 GNP + e$

LUX is another measure of cultural homogeneity: thousands of dollars (U.S.) spent on selected luxury items imported into the Third World. Interpretation of the parameter estimates in Equation [4.3a] (see Table 4.9) indicates that a one-unit increase on the press freedom scale is associated with an average increase in expenditures for imported luxuries of roughly $129 million. A 1 percent increase in imported broadcast media (as a proportion of total broadcasting) is associated with an average increase of $3,321,000 spent on imported luxuries. An increase of $10 in GNP per capita is associated with an average decrease of $110,000 spent on foreign luxury items. However, due to the small sample size, these estimates must be regarded with caution. When we look at the adjusted R^2 (especially important for samples of this size) we find that there is, again, little evidence to support the structural thesis. Only 17 percent of the adjusted variance in luxury imports (adjusted for the size of the sample relative to the number of independent variables in the equation) is associated with the combined variance in press freedom, imported media, and GNP per capita.

The last equation, [4.3b], does provide a relatively good fit for the data (even taking the adjusted R^2 into account), and it also shows some very interesting results (see Table 4.10). CONS is a measure of imported consumer goods as a percentage of total imports. One can see that, within this sample, an increase in GNP per capita of $1,000 is associated with an average increase in imported consumer goods (as a percentage of total imports) of 0.2 percent. But as press freedom and imported media increase,

Table 4.10:
Coefficients for Equation [4.3b]

VARIABLE	UNSTANDARDIZED COEFFICIENT	STANDARDIZED COEFFICIENT	t-RATIO
MI	-.12	-.87	2.79*
PF	-.30	-.09	.32
GNP	.0002	.45	1.45

Dependent Variable = CONS   intercept = 13.27
R^2 = .62   adjusted R^2 = .39   N = 9   s.e. = 2.88

CONS = percentage of imports for consumer goods
(source: United Nations, 1982)
other sources: see Tables 4.1 and 4.2

* = significant at .05

the percentage of imports for consumer goods drops. This is just the opposite of what the structural thesis predicts.

With only nine cases, this sample is admittedly far from ideal. However, data on particular imports are not available for larger numbers of nations. When working with sample sizes this small, caution must be exercised when interpreting the parameters. But even samples of this size can be useful if we note the directions of the relationships involved. Equation 4.3a shows that an increase in GNP per capita is associated with a decrease in the importation of luxuries. As development progresses, some Third World nations begin producing such luxury items domestically and, therefore, importation of these goods decreases (Baer, 1972; Hirschman, 1968; O'Donnell, 1973). Here the tests have produced empirical evidence of Third World nations following the Prebisch thesis. As development advances, Third World nations will tend to move away from the importation of some types of consumer goods and devote more of their resources to purchasing capital and industrial goods from overseas. Import substitution industry then begins to produce goods which were imported at earlier stages of development as one means for breaking some of the dependent ties these nations have to the North.

Equation [4.3b] reveals that as press freedom increases, consumer goods as a percentage of all imports decreases. This relationship is directly contrary to the structural thesis. It is also interesting to note that as imported broadcast media increases, percentages for imported consumer goods tend to decrease, again contrary to the structural thesis. Although the absolute level of spending on foreign luxury items tends to increase along with increases in imported media (as per Equation [4.3a]), consumer goods as a percentage of all imports still tend to decrease.

Unfortunately tests based on H3c cannot be conducted for the Fourth World due to a lack of data. Only five nations would be left in the sample; too few with which to do adequate statistical testing.

Let us now take a step back from the quantitative data to look more closely at the general interactions among the variables. The remainder of this chapter will summarize the interrelationships between advertising, education, imports of consumer goods, press freedom, media imports, and economic development—paying particular attention to the implications these test results hold for validating or disproving the structural thesis of cultural imperialism.

IMPLICATIONS AND CONCLUSIONS FROM THE EMPIRICAL TESTS

Press Freedom as a Possible Cause of Cultural Imperialism

Press freedom is the variable most clearly related to the three areas of westernization (economies, education, and imports). Increased levels of this variable are associated with an increased reliance on market economies and increased use of advertising to stimulate consumption. Because this relationship is statistically significant in the larger sample, one can probably generalize that press freedom and consumer-oriented economies have a positive correlation in the Third World as a whole. Press freedom is also the most important independent variable in its relative ability to account for variance in advertising expenditures. There is further evidence to suggest that higher press freedom is associated with increased expenditures on luxury imports in the Third World as a whole.[18]

In the larger sample, one finds a positive correlation between press freedom and a student drain, but the statistical evidence is too weak to allow for the assumption that this is true of all Third World nations. In the larger sample one also finds a negative correlation between press freedom and the importation of consumer goods as a proportion of total imports. But again, the evidence is too weak to generalize from the sample to all Third World nations.

After we look at the other two independent variables I will assess the probability of a causal link between press freedom and westernization.

Imported Broadcast Media and Westernization

Imported Western media is the most important variable, theoretically, for testing the structural thesis. It is alleged by structuralists to be *the* conduit for Western norms and values and the process of cultural imperialism. It is through imported media that the demonstration effect is said to function.

In the larger sample higher levels of imported media are associated with increased advertising (and therefore consumer economies) and increased importation of luxury goods. Although this is what the structural thesis would predict, the evidence is too weak to suggest that this is true of all Third World nations. Perhaps more important to an assessment of the structural thesis is the fact that media imports are *negatively* correlated with the student drain and the proportional importation of consumer goods. These relationships are in fact the opposite of what the structural thesis maintains. Furthermore, the statistical significance of the media-imports-to-consumer-goods relationship indicates that there may be a negative relationship between these variables in Third World nations as a whole.

Economic Growth and Western Cultural Hegemony

Is it likely that economic development alone leads to a process of westernization in Third World nations as a whole? Evidence from the larger sample suggests that this is in fact not the case. In the sample of twenty-four nations, increased GNP per capita is associated with increases in advertising and the proportional importation of consumer goods. But GNP per capita is negatively correlated with the student drain and importation of luxury items. However, the lack of statistical significance in any one of these relationships indicates that the evidence is too weak to allow generalizations from the sample to the population of Third World nations as a whole.

One could say, on the basis of this evidence alone (and with such mixed results), that economic development (in and of itself) need not necessarily lead to Western modes of business, education, and lifestyles. In other words, the numerous tests provide no evidence that the richest nations of the Third World are necessarily those nations most like the West in terms of these important cultural indicators.

General Conclusions Regarding the Validity of Structural Theory

What, then, do these quantitative studies suggest in regard to the validity of the structural theory of cultural imperialism? There is some support for the structural thesis from the empirical data, if one construes the relationship which clearly exists between press freedom and economic trends to be a causal link. More liberal press policies are associated with a tendency toward consumer-oriented economies. It is also likely that more press freedom is correlated with a trend toward larger expenditures for foreign luxury goods. According to structural theory, there is a causal link between these relationships. Galtung and Schiller would argue that increased press freedom allows more foreign (particularly Western) ideas and media to circulate in the Third World, which in turn stimulate demands for consumer economies and Western luxuries through the demonstration effect. If the causal argument is valid, given the empirical findings, then recommendations by the structuralists regarding control of media as a means to breaking international structures of dependency may also be valid. The structuralists believe that governments which place stricter controls on their print and broadcast media are better able to reduce national expenditures on advertising and luxuries. Media controls are also a means to reduce the brain drain for the structuralist.

On the other hand, the relationship between press freedom and trends of westernization could be a spurious one. It could be that some variable which is exogenous to these tests is determining both press freedom and economic policies. If one looks at government ownership of broadcast media in the Third World, one finds that 100 percent of those nations which have low scores on the press freedom scale and low advertising expenditures also have a system of government ownership.[19] These nations are also almost entirely one-party states located in Africa or Asia. Compare this group with those Third World nations which score high on the press freedom scale and which also have above-average advertising levels. The latter group consists mostly of Latin American states, and only 64 percent of this group have systems of government ownership.[20]

It would seem, therefore, that press freedom may not be tied to westernization in a simple direct causal relationship. Rather, it is possible that those nations which control their media through government ownership are restricting both press freedom and economic policy through direct government intervention. It may be that highly centralized, one-party states are deliberately setting levels of press freedom and advertising at low levels due to their strategies for national development. Before one could ascribe a causal "invisible hand" to a demonstration effect in the Third World, one would have to eliminate the alternative explanation that the "visible hand" of governmental planners in one-party states is really behind the relationship between press freedom and traits of a westernized economy. To do so would require a more in-depth study (perhaps case studies) of those nations which fall into our two separate groups (high press freedom and advertising versus low press freedom and advertising). Such a task will not be taken up at this time, but is one of the directions for further study in which my research points us.

More damaging to structural theory is the fact that Western media, the most important variable in these tests (given their own arguments), show little or no evidence of behaving in the way which structuralists maintain. Furthermore, when one looks at westernization in terms of advertising, or the student drain, or luxury imports, one finds only weak associations to increased media imports. Recall that it is through media imports that the demonstration effect is alleged to primarily function. At the one place within the empirical data at which imported media does show a statistically significant relationship to westernization, it does so in exact opposition to the structural thesis. Increases in media imports tend to lead to *decreases* in the importation of consumer goods (as a proportion of all imports).

Numerous empirical tests have found press freedom and westernization to be clearly related. This is as the structuralists would predict. The preliminary evidence, however, suggests that this may very well be a spurious relationship. Furthermore, one can find little or no evidence in these tests which supports the claim that imported broadcast media lead to westernization. In fact, partial findings indicate that media imports may not be related to westernization at all in the manner which the structural school argues to exist.

Clearly, one needs to have a better understanding of the causal links (or lack thereof) which hold between these processes before the structural thesis can be clearly verified or soundly refuted. Is there a direct link between press freedom and westernization, as structural theory implies? Are there other intervening variables in this process? Is a nation's form of government an exogenous or intervening variable in this process? Similar questions should also be posed for the links between media imports and westernization.

The empirical tests of the structural thesis carried out here are based upon structural theories as they now stand. A major fault with most current structural theories of international relations is that they are painted in such tremendously broad strokes. Structural theorists are not specific enough in their writings to allow researchers of international communication to conduct more rigorous testing of their arguments than I have employed here.

Investigations into the empirical validity of structuralism that employ the methods used here are constrained by several factors. Problems with the availability of data are discussed above. These difficulties are compounded by the historical generalities with which the structuralists prefer to deal. The serial nature of these tests is designed to partially overcome these difficulties. Ideally, one would test specific propositions from structural texts on the entire universe of LDCs. As this is not possible, given the theoretical ambiguities and lack of data, a sample of Third World nations has been subjected to a series of tests based on hypotheses extrapolated from structural writings. No matter how one conceives of cultural imperialism—whether in terms of economic, educational, or consumption trends—one finds little or no evidence that Western cultural hegemony is caused by the media that flow from North to South.

Because this rather extensive series of tests does not give us clear evidence which tends to support the structuralists, one of two conclusions could be drawn. First, one might assume that these arguments have been refuted and hence are false. However, the empirical evidence is not so clear as to allow for such a conclusion (see the discussion in Chapter Six on falsifying theories). Second, one might argue that these tests show the structural arguments to be merely incomplete. If this is the case, structural theorists must admit that they still have a lot of work to do. They must go back to the drawing board and refine their arguments. They need to fill in—with specific details—the causal links in their theories. Structural theorists need to give researchers more to go on (than they have provided up to this point) when studying the relationships which they allege to exist between international communication and development in the Third World.

Cultural Imperialism in the Third World and in the Fourth World

On the basis of the larger sample of twenty-four nations, it would appear that press freedom is more important than economic development in explaining westernization in the Third World as a whole. However, on the basis of the sample of nineteen Fourth World nations, it would seem that economic growth is more important than press freedom in explaining trends toward westernization in the poorest regions of the globe.[21] Are these findings contradictory? Not necessarily.

It would seem that, on the one hand, for the most seriously disadvantaged nations press freedom has little overall importance in the initial push toward westernization. In Fourth World countries a much greater effect is felt from increased economic development. This fact alone tends to introduce westernization. But on the other hand, once a certain point in the developmental process has been reached (I have set this point—somewhat arbitrarily—at a GNP per capita of $2,000), economic development, in and of itself, is not sufficient to lead to further westernization. After a basic level of economic development has been reached, the flow of ideas becomes increasingly important, eclipsing economic growth itself as the mechanism producing westernization.

In conclusion, it would seem that very poor nations which dread cultural imperialism may have more to fear from the first steps toward an industrialized economy than from unrestricted exchanges of news and ideas with the West. Of course, economic development even at these initial levels often carries within it Western modes of analytic thought and the liberal tendency to reduce all cultural and social phenomena to economic terms. Could it be that a partial acceptance of these traits is one of the initial cultural costs paid to acquire the basic fundamentals of economic development? Once these fundamentals are acquired and development is under way, a free flow of news, information, and ideas tends to become more important than sheer economic growth in contributing to further adoption of Western-style economies and lifestyles.

It is also important to reemphasize the fact that imported media from the West—the single most important factor, according to the structural thesis, for shaping Third World nations into the West's image—simply drops out of the explanation entirely.[22] Imported media has no clear relationship to processes of westernization either in the Third World as a whole or within the Fourth World in particular.

NOTES

1. Elie Abel, U.S. representative to the NWIO negotiations, has been quite blunt in his denials of the claim that current markets in international news and information (managed largely by Western interests) have a "negative effect" upon Third World nations (Richstad and Anderson, 1981: 188). For the official U.S. position on the dangers of the NWIO see also U.S. Department of State, 1982 and 1981.

2. I want to conduct a series of tests which will provide the most relevant results in regard to structural theory, given its own arguments (see Note 3 in Chapter Three).

3. I prefer not to follow Galtung's use of the term "brain drain." He uses it to refer to the loss of students to foreign institutions of higher learning. This is a slightly different usage of the term than is most common—using "brain drain" to refer to the loss of already educated specialists to foreign nations (e.g., European scientists who fled to the United States in the 1930s and 1940s). What Galtung is really talking about here is a "student drain," a term I will substitute to refer to the same trends Galtung is dealing with.

4. *Statistics on Radio and Television 1960–1976* (Paris: Unesco, 1978). I have supplemented this data with estimates for imported versus domestic television programming taken from Tapio Varis, "Global Traffic in Television," *Journal of Communication*, 24:1 (1974), 102–109.

5. The Press Freedom Index is taken from George T. Kurian (ed.), *Book of World Rankings* (New York: Facts on File, 1979). This index was created by the University of Missouri School of Journalism, using native and nonnative judges, who ranked each nation on twenty-three items including legal controls on the media, government censorship, favoritism shown for official governmental news (press releases), and governmental control of circulation and distribution. A total of ninety-one countries were ranked on a scale of 4.00 (highest) to -4.00 (lowest). The index consists of the averages of the scores of two native and two nonnative judges. If there was disagreement between the native and nonnative judges of more than 6 percent, judgments of the nonnatives only were used. These rankings apply to the period of the early 1970s.

6. Source: Starch, INRA, Hooper, *Advertising Expenditures Around the World, 1* (New York: Starch, INRA, Hooper, 1982). Data are for 1979.

7. Source: *Unesco Statistical Yearbook* (London: Unesco, 1981). Data are for the year 1978.

8. Source: *1981 Yearbook on International Trade Statistics* (New York: United

Nations, 1982), N = 9. The nine nations are Argentina, Chile, Iraq, Jordan, Lebanon, Mexico, Nigeria, Panama, and Singapore. The luxury items imported include private automobiles, color televisions (for all nations but Mexico), precious and/or imitation jewelry, cosmetics and perfumes (for all nations but Iraq), and yachts (for all nations but Iraq and Jordan). The same source was also used for data on percentages of all imports devoted to consumer goods—or the variable CONS, which appears in Equation [4.3b] and Table 4.10, below.

9. Correlations for these variables are as follows:

Pearson's Correlation Coefficients

	ADV	LOGADV	PF	MI	GNP	EDUC
ADV	1.00	.76	.44	.25	.22	-.25
LOGADV		1.00	.58	.32	.28	-.16
PF			1.00	.17	.14	-.16
MI				1.00	.34	-.21
GNP					1.00	-.03
EDUC						1.00

[N = 24; for LUX and CONS, N = 9 (not included)]

10. Perhaps it would have been better to base the sample on time-series data for each nation rather than on cross-sectional summations of data taken from the past several years. This would give one better grounds on which to argue that certain causal relationships do or do not hold (e.g., that certain phenomena can be shown to follow others chronologically). Unfortunately such data are simply not available. However, cross-sectional data can allow for tests which will show whether or not particular correlations hold between the variables discussed above, as well as the likely directions of these relationships (as being positive or negative). It would also seem that studies such as this could serve as useful (perhaps even necessary) preliminaries to subsequent time-series analyses and case studies.

11. Subsequent equations will include a measure for GNP per capita. Because no nation could actually have a GNP per capita equal to zero, intercept estimates for the following equations have no intuitive meaning, and therefore will not be discussed.

12. Per capita GNP figures were constructed from data taken from Starch, INRA, Hooper and Unesco. Data are for circa 1976.

13. The standardized coefficients (beta weights) for Equation [4.1a] show that variance in advertising accounted for by the variance in press freedom is more than twice that of media imports and nearly four times that of GNP per capita. Thus, when we convert the measures into a single metric, we find that press freedom has by far the most relative importance for explaining differences in advertising expenditures.

14. **Scatterplot of ADV and PF**

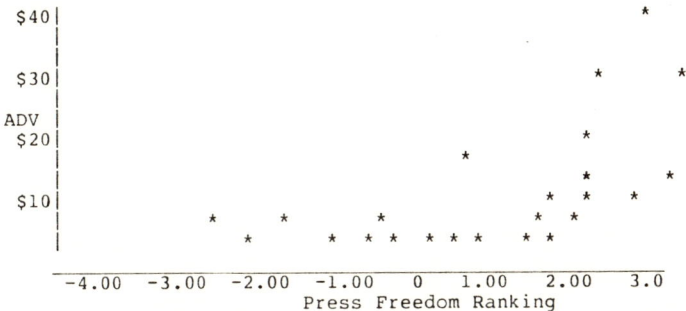

15. Because i = .00 for GNP. Using the formula B = log(1 + i), we find that for PF, i = .70; for MI, i = .012; and for GNP, i = .00. See Tufte, 1974, p. 127.

16. The nations excluded from the smaller sample are Argentina, Chile, Iran, Iraq, and Singapore. The nations which remain all have GNP per capitas of less than $2,000.

17. Equations [4.1] and [4.1b] have already been eliminated from this study due to poor explanatory power.

18. In Equation [4.3a] we find that the t-ratio for press freedom is greater than 2.00 but less than 2.57 (the critical value for the .05 level with five degrees of freedom). This suggests that the relationship between press freedom and imported luxuries may be significant, but a sample with only nine nations is too small to reveal this fact. With additional data and a larger sample size we would probably find this relationship to be statistically significant.

19. These nations are Egypt, Ethiopia, Ghana, Iran, Iraq, Jordan, Nigeria, Pakistan, and Syria.

20. Of this group, Argentina, Brazil, Chile, Colombia, Lebanon, Mexico, and Panama have systems of government ownership. The Dominican Republic, Jamaica, Singapore, and Uruguay do not.

21. Beta weights for Equation [4.1a] for the sample of nineteen nations show that GNP accounts for more of the variance in ADV than does PF: GNP = .66; PF = .18; MI = −.01.

22. Because MI did not load significantly in any of the tests, Equation [4.1c] (the best model) was reestimated without this variable.

Coefficients for Equation [4.1c] without MI

VARIABLE	UNSTANDARDIZED COEFFICIENT	STANDARDIZED COEFFICIENT	t-RATIO
PF	.56	.55	3.17*
GNP	.00007	.20	1.17

Dependent Variable = LOGADV   intercept = .87
R^2 = .38   adjusted R^2 = .32   N = 24   s.e. = 1.26

sources: see Tables 4.1 and 4.2

* = significant at .05

5

Communication and Domestic Violence in the Third World

The term "crisis" has been used in the recent past to characterize several different aspects of the global system of communication. According to Richstad and Anderson, there is a "crisis in international news"; a crisis brought on by factors that contributed to demands for a new order in international communication; a crisis brought to a head by withdrawals from Unesco. Policy studies such as those by Richstad and Anderson (1981) and Coate (1988) address themselves to crises primarily at this level. There is also the "crisis nature *of* international news"; that is, too much crisis-oriented reporting of the type that characterizes a Western media format. Many of the reforms favored by structuralists are designed to address the concept of "crisis" at this level. Finally, there are those theories of individual and group behavior (discussed below) that see a link between media coverage of crisis events—or other forms of media stimulation—and subsequent acts of violence by viewers. Political instability and social unrest in developing nations are thus said to be linked to media exposure and imported (Western) media fare.

The crisis in international news and the crisis nature of international journalism have been treated at length in prior chapters. Here the concern will be on how the form and content of international news and broadcasting may tend to contribute to increased levels of violence in developing nations.

This chapter appeared in *Social Science Quarterly* (March, 1988), 69 (1), under the title "International Information Flows as a Determinant of Political Violence in Third World Nations: Fact or Fiction?" It is reprinted here by permission of the University of Texas Press.

THEORETICAL LINKS BETWEEN MEDIA AND VIOLENCE

Past research on mass media and violence has commonly focused on the possibility that portrayals of violence in television and film lead to violent behavior on the part of people who view this material. Such research, conducted largely by psychologists, has been concerned with the violent messages carried through mass media (e.g., acts of violence, racism and exploitation). These researchers have tried to establish the nature of the relationship between violence on the screen and subsequent violent behavior by members of the audience. The problem of mass media inducing violence is conceptualized in terms of imitation, increased aggressiveness, and changes in attitude "caused" by exposure to too much violence. Courts have even been forced to deal with this argument when it has been put forth as grounds for a legal defense (i.e., diminished capacity due to overexposure to violence in the media).

Does violence in the media lead to violent behavior on the part of those who view it? The results of psychological studies are mixed on this point (see Halloran, 1980, for a summary). In any event, this is not the relationship with which this discussion will be concerned. Although the effects of mass media have been extensively analyzed on this level, little or no study has been done on the role mass media play internationally in contributing to increased (or decreased) levels of violence. A Unesco-sponsored symposium of media specialists, sociologists, psychologists, social workers and educators claimed to be the first attempt to address this issue on an international level in 1970 (see Burnet, 1971). Halloran, in discussing the few scattered and partial studies conducted since that time, argues that past research on media and violence has been largely misdirected. Speaking of the thesis that scenes of violence in the media produce violent tendencies in those who are exposed to this material, Halloran goes on to say that "the media do have influence [on violence in society] but not primarily in this way" (1980: 439). Halloran argues that we should turn our attention toward the role that mass media play in increasing feelings of frustration and dissatisfaction that, in turn, lead to violent acts.

Another recent trend in media research has been to study the coverage of terrorism (Altheide, 1987; Carpini and Williams, 1987). Hijackings, the taking of hostages, and similar terror tactics are often tailored to maximize media coverage. Television serves as a means for terrorists to publicize their causes, and mass media have come under criticism for indirectly promoting violence of a "performance" nature. Terrorists understand very well the commodity character of Western news (described in Chapter Two). They know what sells in the spot news market: primarily reports of violence and crises. During a terrorist incident, average newspaper circulation increases by 35 percent and television news ratings increase as much, if not more (Schmid and deGraff, 1982: 34–35). In fact, terrorists *rely* on the spot nature of international journalism when planning and executing their paramilitary operations. However, this sort of "episodic" violence, and its possible causal link to mass media, is another area only indirectly addressed by the research presented here. I am more interested in the likelihood that media may promote more "endemic" forms of violence in the Third World.

Endemic or chronic violence of the sort quantified below is subtler and relatively harder to locate than is the episodic violence (terrorism) that garners much greater media attention. By endemic violence I mean racial and ethnic unrest that results from feelings of deprivation and frustration. Endemic violence is more pervasive than episodic violence in ethnically divided less developed countries (LDCs) in the sense that it is almost always present to some extent (unlike acts of terrorism). While it may find momentary expression in such overt acts as food riots and racial unrest, even when it is not visible in this way, the underlying emotions that stimulate endemic violence remain. The fear expressed by Halloran and others is that we may overlook the possibility of mass media inducing endemic violence. To focus on media promoting violence in the forms of imitation and performance may blind us to the link between mass media and endemic violence in underprivileged nations.

Third World leaders place a high priority on mass media policies. As a rule, one of the first acts of each newly independent nation in the postwar period was to create media policies consciously designed to increase feelings of national unity and national identification (Katz and Wedell, 1977: 35). There was a pervasive feeling within these new nations that they "must try to unite different ethnic and linguistic groups and give them a sense of national identity" (Burnet, 1971: 31). Broadcasting was designed to help overcome subnational identifications (e.g., ethnic divisions) and to instill an overarching sense of national unity. Foreign control of radio and television was ended. Efforts were made to increase the coverage of broadcasting so that the whole population of a given nation could be reached (at least by radio broadcasts). Efforts were also made to decrease the prices of receivers so that more people could afford to hear and see these broadcasts. To emphasize the sense of national unity, European languages were replaced with a national language. The theme of unity was also personified by giving a great deal of air time to national leaders and office holders who ostensibly represented all the people. In nations such as Tanzania and Senegal, radio broadcasting was used to create links between the urban center and the rural periphery. The primary function of television in nations such as Nigeria was to help solve the problems of national integration. It was hoped that these steps would make the people of such nations see themselves as (for example) Nigerians rather than as Iboes or Fulanis or Yorubas (see Katz and Wedell, 1977: Chapters 1 and 6).

After one or two decades of independence, however, many Third World leaders realized that mass media have the potential to divide a nation as efficiently, and perhaps more quickly, than they can unite a people. Early attempts at nation-building fell far short of the hopes of Third World leaders. Early postwar attempts at economic development and political integration were often woefully inadequate. NWIO advocates have cited the divisive potential of some media fare as a primary reason that developing nations need media policies and media controls which are fundamentally different from the free-press institutions of the West. According to Unesco,

Not suprisingly, *many developing countries stress the role of the media in promoting national development and national identity but complain that* existing patterns of ownership and control and *the importation of media material* representing different cultural values not only do not facilitate this but *actively prevent it*. (Burnet, 1971: 38, emphasis added)

FRUSTRATIONS, AGGRESSIONS, AND VIOLENCE IN DEVELOPING NATIONS

There has long been a recognition within the international community that political unrest in one state could be induced via information from external sources. The Nazis made this fact the basis of many of their early propaganda campaigns (aimed at inciting Germanic peoples in other states). Nazi policies represent the extreme case: propaganda transmitted across national borders to incite ethnic or racial violence. Steps have been taken to eliminate these types of propaganda from international affairs (McPhail, 1987: Appendix B). Third World leaders, however, are also concerned with subtler ways by which inputs of foreign information can lead to political violence. To understand these concerns we need to review the types of information inputs LDCs receive from the West, as well as the political and economic contexts of the former group of nations. It is within these contexts that the comparatively subtle mechanism of the "demonstration effect" is said to raise levels of frustration and, therefore, produce domestic violence.

Third World nations often suffer from severely limited resources. These are also nations which are marked by many ethnic divisions, particularly in much of Asia and sub-Saharan Africa. Western media fare transmitted or imported into these nations carries images of prosperity and material wealth. Western programming portrays more comfortable and exciting ways of life. From these it is alleged that a demonstration effect raises the expectations of Third World peoples. Advertising is a crucial element in this argument, as it was in regard to the claims concerning cultural imperialism (see Chapter Four). By its very nature, advertising increases the expectations and desires of the peoples of the Third World. Halloran points out that "one of the tasks of advertising is to make people dissatisfied with what they have and to stimulate them to want more, irrespective of their economic circumstances" (1980: 437). These conditions lead to increased demands on the political systems to meet the material wants of the people of developing nations.

Because Third World politics is often the politics of ethnicity (i.e., political divisions follow ethnic cleavages), demands are channeled to the government via subnational groups. Because national resources are severly limited, this is also often a zero-sum game. Therefore, conflict escalates between these subnational ethnic parties which are in competition for scarce resources. As each ethnic party demands more of the limited resources, intra-group identities and cohesion are reinforced while intergroup political conflict increases. Subnational identities are reinforced and attempts by national leaders to promote an overarching national identity fail. Once violence between these groups breaks out, it often feeds on itself. According to Burnet, "Presentation of violence in the news may magnify the frustration felt by all members of the group concerned [in the news report], whether or not they as individuals were involved" (1971: 16).

Theories linking frustration to aggression date back as far as the interwar studies of John Dollard and others at Yale. In discussing the "frustration-aggression theory," Dougherty and Pfaltzgraff point out that there is "a convincing body of experimental evidence" to support the theory at the micro-level (e.g., as an explanation for aggression by individuals). Even though this hypothesis may have been verified for individuals and small groups, however, "it would seem much more difficult, and perhaps impossible to apply the theory in any precise way to the behavior of larger, more highly institutionalized social entities" (1981, 269–270).

Doughtery and Pfaltzgraff fault Dollard for moving from the microcosmic to the macrocosmic level "more by logical inference than by experimentation," and "without expressing any doubt as to the validity of the transfer [or] offering any substantiating evidence or argument that the transfer can in fact be made" (1981, 269–271). These authors would also criticize those who argue that rising expectations combined with economic frustrations produce political unrest in LDCs for not supporting their claims with "any careful analysis of the psychological processes involved" (p. 266). They go on to cite several reasons why the move from micro- to macro-levels may not be justifiable.[1]

Despite the theoretical problems inherent in the frustration-aggression thesis (e.g., the possibility of commiting an "ecological fallacy"), there are still two considerations that indicate a need for empirically testing this theory. First, several recent theories of LDC political and economic development lean heavily upon some version of this thesis.[2] Second, this argument has an important *political* status, apart from its theoretical merits or faults. A great deal of weight has been ascribed to these theories in many policy debates in international political forums. This brings us back to matters closer at hand.

At several points in her report from the Unesco symposium on violence, Burnet relates the "dangers" that developing countries see in "alien media materials." Audiences in LDCs allegedly are led to believe that "the change to a more 'advanced' society can be made simply by adopting its surface modes of behavior, its gadgets and status symbols." Hence "the astonishing number of television sets, high fidelity radios and oversize refrigerators counted in a shanty town." Furthermore, alien media "may lead to frustration because audiences cannot acquire these status symbols, or live in the comparatively luxurious way that is shown on the screen" (1971: 32–33). Elsewhere, Burnet points out that

> quite aside from any representation of violence ... the content of the media in general, and of television in particular may arouse or reinforce feelings of frustration by an emphasis on materialistic aims which is not by any means confined to advertising matter. By showing to the disadvantaged visions of luxuries beyond their reach or by holding out goals which to them seem unattainable (except, perhaps, by violence), television constantly reminds these sections of the audience of what they lack, and stimulates achievement drives which are new sources of frustration. (p. 21)

Halloran makes a similar point, linking Western media material to rising frustrations in these deprived nations, and then goes on to make the tie from this process to subsequent domestic violence more explicit.

> In these circumstances, deprived groups in society are reminded, by a daily bombardment, of what is available to others, what is said to be theirs for the asking, yet what they certainly do not possess and, moreover, are not likely ever to achieve. There are, of course, other powerful agents of frustration operating at a variety of levels, from the interpersonal to the environmental, but it would be foolish to ignore the possibility that media, in their normal day-to-day operations, by the presentation of these norms and values, may increase expectations unrealistically, aggravate existing problems, contribute to frustration and consequently to the aggression and violence that may stem from this. (p. 437)

Halloran is at pains to point out that this is an area in which research is desperately needed, but which is also, unfortunately, "not the sort of relationship people normally have in mind when they speculate or pontificate about the link between the media and violence" (*ibid.*). This is, however, precisely the area addressed by the following research.

CONFLICTING POLICY PROPOSALS

Many of those who argue that Western media content contributes to increased violence in developing nations believe that LDCs should restrict the inflows of such material. They would recommend that Third World nations prevent "dependency" on such media through curtailing their importation and through close governmental regulation of the press and broadcasting industries. If these arguments are sound, then LDCs should experience less internal political unrest by means of restricting media imports and tight media regulation. If these policies were found to be effective, then NWIO advocates would have evidence to support their policy proposals.

On the other hand, we have the arguments put forth by the opponents of the NWIO, which are drawn from traditional liberal democratic political theory, favoring the free flow of information internationally (Merrill, 1981; Sussman, 1981b). This school of thought argues that free speech and an international free flow of information can actually help to decrease political violence in the Third World. Imported media is said to contribute to the free exchange of ideas. Freedom of expression is said to open up alternatives, show new possibilities, and promote contacts between developed and developing nations for their mutual benefit. Increased mass media exposure for the peoples of LDCs is therefore a primary source of political and economic innovation (Apter, 1965: 45). Lerner (1964: 62-63) believes that there is a "systemic interdependence" between increased mass media exposure and increased political participation. Furthermore, political participation (e.g., voting, campaigning) is the essential equivalent of political development for Apter, Lerner, and their followers because it may prevent illegitimate (violent) political action.

There is a liberal democratic bias in favor of free expression largely because of the belief that it can temper hostilities and divert potentially violent political behavior. Stretching back at least as far as John Stuart Mill is a Western political tradition which argues that freedom of expression serves as a political alternative to violence. On these grounds, free discussion is seen as a way to defuse a violent situation. Any efforts to restrict free expression or to close off debate on key political issues is seen as depriving society "of its chief non-violent means of self-improvement" (Burnet, 1971: 10).

If developing nations that support the free flow by importing foreign media and by allowing greater press freedom are also the LDCs which tend to be stabler politically (i.e., lower levels of violence), then these facts would tend to support liberal arguments in favor of a free flow. Conversely, if nations with lower levels of imported media and press freedom tend to have stabler political systems, then this would tend to imply that NWIO advocates of a regulated flow are right, and NWIO policies

Figure 5.1:
Specification of the Violence Thesis

DEPENDENT VARIABLE(S)	INDEPENDENT VARIABLE(S)
H1 Frustration-Aggression	= f(Media Dependency)
H2 Domestic Violence	= f(Media Imports, Press Freedom)
H2/Equation [5.1] INDEX A	= a + B_1MI + B_2PF + e

INDEX A = index of political violence
MI = media imported
PF = press freedom
a = constant (intercept)
e = error term

may be more effective in creating a sense of national identity while reducing political conflict. A series of empirical tests will show which of these two camps is supported by the best available data.

SPECIFYING THE VIOLENCE THESIS

Figure 5.1 contains three specifications (of increasing precision) of the thesis that ties international communication to violence in developing nations. Hypothesis H1 states that frustration-induced aggressions are a function of dependency on foreign (Western) media. Hypothesis H2 puts the same argument into more specific terms. It states that domestic violence in the Third World is a function of media imports and press freedom. H2 is expressed even more precisely in Equation [5.1].

The Variables

The remaining tests employ the methodology outlined in the preceding chapter.[3] We want to know what the relationship is between imported media and press freedom (on the one hand) and political violence in the Third World (on the other hand). The determining variables of media imports (MI) and press freedom (PF) will be operationalized as in Chapter Four. Alternate tests will control for levels of wealth, social inequality, and ethnic heterogeneity, as these are factors that may be other determinants of political unrest in LDCs, independent of media trends.

The dependent variable in this model must provide an accurate measure

Table 5.1:
Coefficients for Equation [5.1a]

VARIABLE	UNSTANDARDIZED COEFFICIENT	STANDARDIZED COEFFICIENT	t- RATIO
MI	-.67	-.09	.51
PF	-49.0	-.42	2.45*
GNP	.02	.60	3.36*

Dependent Variable = INDEX A   intercept = 4.63
R^2 = .44   adjusted R^2 = .36   N = 24   s.e. = 143

INDEX A = index of violence
    (source: Taylor and Jodice, 1983)
  MI = media imported
    (source: Unesco, 1978)
  PF = press freedom on an 8-point scale
    (source: Kurian, 1979)
  GNP = gross national product per capita
    (source: Unesco, 1978; and Starch, INRA, Hooper, 1982)

* = significant at .05 level, two-tailed test

of political instability or unrest. Political unrest will be my indicator of that process in which frustrations are said to lead to aggression. The first means of operationalizing the dependent variable is an index that represents the sum total of all protest demonstrations, riots, political strikes, political executions, and government sanctions in the 1970s.[4] By combining these particular measures of unrest, we have an index that gauges violence by the population against the government (e.g., demonstrations, riots, and strikes) as well as acts of coercion by the government against the people (e.g., executions and sanctions).

TESTING THE VIOLENCE THESIS

Rather than beginning the tests by estimating Equation [5.1], a measure of development (GNP per capita) has been entered into Equation [5.1a] to control for the possible effects that economic conditions may have on domestic violence, independent of media policies:[5]

H2/Equation [5.1a]   INDEX A = $a + B_1 MI + B_2 PF + B_3 GNP + e$

Equation [5.1a] states that levels of political violence in Third World nations are a function of press freedom, imported media, and economic development.[6] An inverse relationship exists between press freedom and violence (see Table 5.1). A one-unit increase on the press freedom (PF) scale is associated with an average decrease of forty-nine acts of political violence (independent of media imports [MI] and GNP). Contrast this with the positive correlation between growth in GNP per capita and higher levels of political violence. An increase of $500 in GNP per capita would be associated with an average increase of ten acts of political violence (independent of PF and MI). Because both of these slope estimates are statistically significant, one can reject the null hypothesis and assert that these relationships hold for the twenty-four nations sampled. Media imports also have an inverse relationship to political violence in the sample. However, the lack of statistical significance in this parameter does not allow for a rejection of the null hypothesis. Equation [5.1a] does provide a good fit for the empirical data, with 44 percent of the variance in political violence accounted for by the combined variance in PF, MI, and GNP.

Of course, there are other factors that may provoke political violence in Third World nations, factors that have been left out of the first test. Two of the more obvious candidates would be social inequality and ethnic heterogeneity. As inequality or ethnic differences increase, one might expect political violence to increase as well. One can control for the effects of these additional variables by incorporating measures of each into alternate model specifications. Equations [5.1b] and [5.1c] control for inequality[7] and ethnic heterogeneity,[8] respectively:

H2/Equation [5.1b]:

$$\text{INDEX A} = a + B_1 MI + B_2 PF + B_3 GNP + B_4 GINI + e$$

H2/Equation [5.1c]:

$$\text{INDEX A} = a + B_1 MI + B_2 PF + B_3 GNP + B_4 ED + e$$

When controlling for inequality (measured via the GINI index; see Table 5.2) or for ethnic divisions (the heterogeneity measure ED; see Table 5.3), there is relatively little change in the partial slope estimates for PF and GNP. The small change in the estimates, combined with the fact that PF and GNP retain statistical significance when other variables are added or dropped, increases one's confidence in the initial conclusions. That is, it supports the claim that one can reject the null hypothesis of no relationship and maintain that press freedom is negatively correlated with political violence while economic development is positively correlated with political violence. Inclusion of the GINI index of inequality (Table 5.2) adds little explanatory power to the model. This variable is not statistically significant, and including it raises the multiple coefficient of determination only slightly.

Inclusion of the ethnic division measure, ED (Table 5.3), gives the model the best fit yet to the data. Almost half of the variance in political violence can be accounted for by the combined variance of the independent variables in [5.1c]. However, because ED is also not statistically significant, no firm

Table 5.2:
Coefficients for Equation [5.1b]

VARIABLE	UNSTANDARDIZED COEFFICIENT	STANDARDIZED COEFFICIENT	t-RATIO
MI	-.48	-.06	.35
PF	-53.0	-.45	2.49*
GNP	.02	.58	3.22*
GINI	-1.04	-.11	.63

Dependent Variable = INDEX A intercept = 183
R^2 = .46 adjusted R^2 = .34 N = 24 s.e. = 145

GINI = index of landed inequality
(source: Taylor and Jodice, 1983)
other sources: see Table 5.1

* = significant at .05

Table 5.3:
Coefficients for Equation [5.1c]

VARIABLE	UNSTANDARDIZED COEFFICIENT	STANDARDIZED COEFFICIENT	t-RATIO
MI	-.64	-.09	.49
PF	-47.0	-.40	2.33*
GNP	.03	.64	3.54*
ED	1.17	.20	1.18

Dependent Variable = INDEX A intercept = 99
R^2 = .48 adjusted R^2 = .37 N = 24 s.e. = 142

ED = ethnic division measure (source: Kurian, 1984)
other sources: see Table 5.1

* = significant at .05

conclusions can be drawn from the sample about its relationship to political violence.

As one final test of the thesis that links international communication to political unrest in LDCs, another factor has been substituted as the means for measuring the dependent variable. Instead of looking at political violence as a "two-way street"—measured as both violence by the people against the political system (riots and demonstrations) and as coercion by the government against the people (executions and sanctions)—violence could be conceptualized in terms of a "one-way street." The second index of political violence, used in Equation [5.2], is the sum of violent acts by the people against the status quo. INDEX B does not include coercive acts

Table 5.4:
Coefficients for Equation [5.2]

VARIABLE	UNSTANDARDIZED COEFFICIENT	STANDARDIZED COEFFICIENT	t-RATIO
MI	-.70	-.28	1.22
PF	-6.5	-.16	.73
GNP	.004	.26	1.14
ED	.27	.13	.63

Dependent Variable = INDEX B intercept = 65
R^2 = .14   adjusted R^2 = -.04   N = 24   s.e. = 63

sources: see Tables 5.1 and 5.5

---

by the government. In addition to riots, demonstrations, and strikes, however, it does include successful and unsuccessful coups d'etat, which are weighted to account for their relative importance as a measure of violence against the status quo.[9] Equation [5.2] uses this new indicator for the dependent variable, but retains the indicators from Equation [5.1c] for the independent variables. You will recall that these indicators provided the best model for the data.

H2/Equation [5.2]:
$$\text{INDEX B} = a + B_1 MI + B_2 PF + B_3 GNP + B_4 ED + e$$

As one can see from Table 5.4, Equation [5.2] does not provide as good of a model of political violence as did the three previous equations. None of the parameters are statistically significant, and this model accounts for very little of the variance in Third World political unrest. However, it is important to note that the direction of each relationship is the same for Equations [5.1c] and [5.2]. *Even when operationalizing political violence by use of a very different index*, the finding is that there are still positive correlations between violence and GNP or ED; and there are negative correlations between violence and PF or MI. The tests have now reached a point where their implications (drawn specifically from the equation with the best fit, [5.1c]) for the arguments linking political violence to international communication can be summarized.

CONCLUSIONS AND IMPLICATIONS

Press Freedom as a Tool for Political Stability

The empirical research shows that as levels of press freedom increase, political violence in developing nations tends to decrease. This relationship characterizes all four of the equations discussed in this chapter. Here the test results directly support liberal arguments in favor of a free flow of ideas and a free exchange of viewpoints as means for reducing violent political conflict. It seems that the most effective policy for LDCs divided by ethnic cleavages may be to promote freedom of expression for all such groups as a way to increase understanding of one another. These findings are consistent with the argument that as more expression is allowed, political violence tends to abate. There is a positive association between increasing press freedom and increasing domestic stability.

Some of the participants at the Unesco symposium on mass media and violence supported this view, including a few of the representatives from developing countries. According to one speaker from Asia, mass media had helped to decrease political violence in her nation, and "by counteracting false rumours, had helped reduce violence between ethnic groups" (Burnet, 1971: 32). In the official Summary Statement released by Unesco after the conclusion of the symposium, these considerations were incorporated into the recommendations made by that body for media policies in the Third World:

On a more specific point, *the media, recognizing that there is violence and conflict in society, might give more attention to deliberate attempts to* foster comprehension of the phenomenon, facilitate a resolution of the conflict and *promote understanding among divergent social groups and nations.* (Emphasis added; see Burnet, 1971: Appendix 1)

Economic Development and Trends Toward Political Violence

Turning now to economic development, this research has shown that the more prosperous Third World nations tend to experience higher levels of political violence. This is another relationship which held up throughout the entire series of empirical tests. GNP per capita is also the most important variable in these tests in terms of its relative ability to account for variance in the dependent variables (the indices of violence).[10] It would seem that, as the stakes of the political game increase, the tendency to use violent methods to gain the political spoils also increases. This would be especially true if the political contest was a zero-sum game (as it often is in LDCs). With more national wealth at stake, if the game is one of winner-take-all, there is a much stronger incentive to raise the ante, with violence if necessary, in the hopes that this will keep as many players (e.g., ethnic groups) out of the game as possible.

Western Media and Political Violence in the Third World

Western media is the variable which carries the most theoretical import for the supporters of the NWIO. It was charged at the same Unesco symposium that alien (Western) media contribute to increased violence in the Third World. This is argued to come about through the demonstration effect which raises the aspirations and frustrations of the people of developing nations. These frustrations are said to be the source of new violence on the part of the disadvantaged. However, after empirically testing this argument, one finds that imported media virtually drops out of the explanation altogether.[11]

These empirical analyses have yielded no evidence to support the thesis that increasing media imports lead to increasing levels of violence in the developing nations. Throughout the tests of Third World violence as a function of modernization and mass media, the consistent finding is that media imports have no significant relationship to increased violence. Therefore, these tests give one no grounds on which to reject the claim that there is no relationship between imported media and Third World violence. Media imported is also the least important variable in Equation [5.1c] in its ability to explain the variance in levels of Third World violence. Perhaps just as damaging to the arguments that call for controls to keep Western media out of developing nations is the fact that, within the twenty-four nations sampled, the relationship between imported media and political violence is just the opposite of what structuralists and NWIO advocates would predict. As media imports increase across these nations, levels of political unrest tend to drop.

NOTES

1. Among these considerations are the different time factors involved between this process at an individual as opposed to a societal level; the variance in individuals' perceptions of frustrating situations; variance in responses to frustration among individuals; the culture-specific nature of frustration to aggressions; and the increased difficulty in verifying the hypothesis at the level of large-group behavior (see pp. 270–271).

2. A prime example is O'Donnell's theory of bureaucratic authoritarianism. According to O'Donnell, in the historical process of modernization in LDCs, development began in earnest and expectations rose quickly during a relatively short period of rapid postwar industrialization. This "take-off" to development was interrupted in most cases, however, due to a number of reasons (e.g., international economic recessions, increased importation of consumer goods which dried up local investment capital). Third World governments then found themselves unable to sustain popular need satisfaction. Fears that a sense of relative deprivation would make the masses prone to revolts led rulers of many LDCs to adopt more repressive and authoritarian measures (see O'Donnell, 1973).

Theories such as that of O'Donnell also point to the importance of including measures of governmental repression/violence into any adequate indicator of political violence in Third World nations (in addition to measures of violence by the masses such as riots and demonstrations; see the discussion of INDEX A, below).

3. For those wishing to review the rationale behind the indicators for the independent variables, see the section on operationalization in Chapter Four; for arguments supporting my sampling techniques, see the section on the sample in the same chapter.

4. Charles Lewis Taylor and David A. Jodice, *World Handbook of Political and Social Indicators* (New Haven, Conn.: Yale University Press, 1983), vol. II. A protest demonstration is defined as a "gathering of people organized for the announced purpose of protesting against a regime or government" (p. 19). A political strike is a "work stoppage by a body of industrial or service workers or a stoppage of normal academic life by students to protest a regime" (p. 21). A riot is any "demonstration or disturbance that becomes violent" (p. 29). A government sanction is defined as "an action taken by the authorities to neutralize, suppress or eliminate a perceived threat to the security of the government," such as declarations of martial law, banning or harassing political parties and exiling people for engaging in political actions (pp. 62–63). "Typically, a political execution is one in which the person executed is charged with activities threatening the security of the state." Excluded are executions for criminal offenses (p. 63). Totals are for 1970–1977, inclusive.

I have constructed an index of the items above in order to give a more accurate and complete indication of levels of political violence in these nations. I feel that a measure that reflects many types of political unrest is (in theory) a better gauge of overall socio-political violence than an indicator based on just one form of turmoil. Such an index is therefore more directly relevant to the arguments I am testing as well.

5. The indicators for the independent and dependent variables are taken from the same general time-frame. They are meant to provide a cross-sectional sketch of media policies and the gross levels of violence in LDCs from the middle to late 1970s. Violence data are for 1970–1977. Data on media imports are for 1972–1975 (using the most recent years reported). Data on press freedom are for the early 1970s. GNP estimates are circa 1976. The GINI index and the ethnic heterogeneity measures (used in later tests) are for 1970 and the period of 1960 to 1965, respectively. For more information see Chapter Four, Note 10, and for sources see Table 5.1.

6. Correlations for variables employed:

Pearson's Correlation Coefficients

	INDEX A	INDEX B	PF	MI	GNP	ED	GINI
INDEX A	1.00	-.39	-.35	.04	.51	.13	-.05
INDEX B		1.00	-.19	-.23	.12	.13	-.29
PF			1.00	.17	.14	-.14	-.25
MI				1.00	.34	-.10	.15
GNP					1.00	-.21	-.07
ED						1.00	.32
GINI							1.00

7. GINI Coefficient of Land Inequality taken from Taylor and Jodice, vol. I, pp. 140–141.

8. George Thomas Kurian, *The New Book of World Rankings* (New York: Facts on File, 1984), pp. 47–49.

9. Taylor and Jodice, vol. II. Again, totals are for 1970–1977. Successful and unsuccessful coups (listed in vol. II as irregular executive transfers and unsuccessful irregular executive transfers) are multiplied by a factor of ten to account for their relative weight in gauging political unrest. In practical terms, this means that I am assuming that a coup is roughly ten times as important as a riot in measuring the public's discontent with a regime. In INDEX A, no variable was weighted in this manner. There I have assumed that the variables combined in the index are of roughly equal value as measures of political violence. That is, I assumed a rough equivalency among riots, strikes, demonstrations, and so forth, an assumption which does not seem valid when factoring in regime changes.

10. Standardized coefficients for Equation [5.1c]: GNP = .64; PF = −.40; ED = .20; MI = −.09.

11. Because MI did not load significantly in any of the tests, Equation [5.1c] (the best model) was reestimated without this variable:

Coefficients for Equation [5.1c] without MI

VARIABLE	UNSTANDARDIZED COEFFICIENT	STANDARDIZED COEFFICIENT	t-RATIO
PF	−48.6	−.41	2.48*
GNP	.03	.61	3.63*
ED	1.18	.20	1.21

Dependent Variable = INDEX A intercept = 84
R^2 = .48   adjusted R^2 = .40   N = 24   s.e. = 140

sources: see Tables 5.1 and 5.3

* = significant at .05

6

International Relations Theory and Communication Policy

This investigation has taken as its point of departure several claims advanced by advocates of a New World Information Order (NWIO). These policy-oriented claims are drawn to a large extent from the postulates of structuralists such as Johan Galtung and Herbert Schiller, and from *dependencia* (dependency) theorists such as Fernando Cardoso and Enzo Faletto.[1] Once Unesco policy debates had been placed into the theoretical context of liberal versus structural theories of Third World development, data analysis was employed to assess the validity of claims supporting the NWIO. In conclusion, I would like to return to the prior theoretical and policy issues by putting the discrete empirical studies into a more comprehensive perspective. The best directions for further research on international communication and Third World development will also be outlined.

IMPLICATIONS OF THE COMBINED TESTS FOR STRUCTURAL THEORY

Chapter Three investigated claims regarding alleged imbalances in international communication, alleged biased reporting about developing nations in the Western press, and the structure of international news flows. In regard to the first claim, aggregate data from Unesco showed that LDCs do rely on the West for a large portion of television programming. A news flow study of Africa and Latin America showed that the same is largely true for international news reports. The claim of dependency was found to be invalid, however, if applied to radio programming. With respect to the second claim (biased reporting by Western media), Western and non-Western papers were found to be similar in their coverage of regions and topics. However, additional evidence showed that reports taken from Big

Four agencies (AFP, AP, Reuters, UPI) did focus more on spot reports of unrest and violence, while items taken from nonaligned agencies were likely to contain more developmental news. Despite these trends, however, the African and Latin American dailies still exhibited a heavy reliance on Big Four releases for timely international reports.

This reliance upon Western transnational news agencies (TNNAs) is denied to be an "imbalance" by some (Stevenson and Cole, 1980) because they have found that the Big Four supply a great deal of Latin American news to their Latin American customers, African news to African markets, and so forth. Schramm (1980: 593) also points out that Third World papers are all basically "regional" papers. Surely such rebuttals miss the point. Of course TNNAs provide news about a given region to dailies in that area. The discussion of news as a commodity in Chapter Two should lead one to realize that this is to be expected. Western news is news as a commodity. It is news tailored to the consumer tastes of each market. Therefore, TNNA services to Latin America carry mostly Latin American news, and so on. This does not alter the fact that resource-poor nonaligned agencies are unable to cover the globe (as the TNNAs do). Lack of economic resources creates a situation in which Third World editors may be forced into a heavy reliance upon TNNA services, despite the fact that stories from the Big Four consisted of mostly spot reports with very little developmental news.

On the third topic of Chapter Three, there is strong evidence to support the structural claim that international information flows follow neocolonial routes. News flow studies indicate that the wire service of a former colonial power has a favored status in delivering news to its ex-colonies. News flowing out of former French colonies is channeled primarily via AFP; news inputs and outputs to and from former British colonies are channeled mainly through Reuters; and so on.

Chapters Four and Five investigated the structural hypothesis that a demonstration effect stimulated by imported, Western media creates conditions of cultural imperialism and domestic unrest in Third World nations. The research of Chapter Four shows that, contrary to prior claims, higher levels of media imports are not associated with a stronger tendency toward economic, educational, or lifestyle westernization in LDCs. Rather, westernization is associated either with increasing economic growth (in the poorest of nations) or with increasing press freedom. Furthermore, increasing levels of imported media across LDCs are not associated with higher levels of domestic violence. Chapter Five revealed correlations between increased economic growth and more political disturbances, and between decreasing press freedom and political instability. There is no evidence to suggest, however, that increasing importation of Western media is correlated with increasing Third World political unrest.

NEOIMPERIAL INFORMATION FLOWS: STRUCTURE VERSUS IMPACT

Perhaps the most significant conclusion that can be drawn from these inquiries into global communication, and certainly the one with the greatest theoretical import, is the fact that structuralism is correct when used as a model of global information flows, but it is only partially correct. Structural theorists are only half-right. Galtung's description of a world marked by neocolonial and vertical information flows is an accurate portrayal. The news flow evidence from Chapter Three confirms as much. However, NWIO supporters and structural theorists (e.g., Schiller) who want to go further, claiming that cultural imperialism is one of the necessary effects of the neocolonial flow, have little or no empirical support on which to stand.

Does the current international regime in information flows, a regime created and controlled largely by Western interests, constitute a neoimperial system? Clearly, this is the case. But does this system also lead to westernization and domestic instability in the Third World? The best available evidence indicates that this is not the case. Neocolonialism works well as a rough description or blueprint of global interactions, but structural communication theory is much less accurate when it attempts to delineate the impact of the system on developing nations. Although the structuralists have drawn us an accurate picture of the global information "machine," they have not given us a valid account of the work this machine produces in the LDCs. The one does not necessarily follow from the other.

The value of structural theory of international communication lies primarily in its ability to describe the framework of information flows and the nature of North-South relations in general. When structuralism, at least in its current stage of development, is pushed beyond this level and attempts to offer causal explanations of political and economic change in LDCs, when it tries to make connections from the international to the national and subnational levels, its utility and accuracy wane. The precise effects of global communication on particular LDCs is an area in which the structural school has yet to develop the concepts or the research tools and techniques that are necessary elements of any valid causal explanation.

As international communication flows are distinctly neoimperial in nature, one would certainly expect to find some sort of pernicious systemic effects within Third World nations. The privation of sovereignty (in the Third World) which the system entails is something that few advanced industrialized (Western) powers would tolerate. LDCs of the South are expected (by defenders of the status quo) to accept willingly this partial loss of national independence because it is one of the "dictates" of the global marketplace. Structuralism has attempted to go further in detailing the damages that the international information regime has inflicted upon LDCs, an attempt that has yet to achieve its goal. In this one respect, however, structuralism does not differ to any large extent from notable and prior theories of international relations.

Systems theory is a body of work more highly regarded in most Western academic circles than is the neo-Marxist work of structuralism. Given their divergent political ideologies (marxian versus liberal), it is more than a little ironic to find interesting parallels between the work of Johan Galtung, on the one hand, and the international systems theories of Morton Kaplan (1975) or Kenneth Waltz (1979), on the other hand. Speaking in those terms which have been used to critique systems theory, Galtung's structural theory of international relations is most accurate when it uses the concept of "Structure-as-Description." This is also the most accurate use of the systemic theories of Kaplan and Waltz, that is, when one uses the concept of "System-as-Description" (Goodman, 1965: 258). When one tries to use either concept, that of "structure" or that of "system," so as to construct *causal* models, the truth-value and utility of both theoretical schools decline rapidly. Although the concept of "Structure-as-Explanation" currently has little theoretical validity, many would charge that the same could be said of the concept of "System-as-Explanation" (cf. Goodman, 1965: Part II).

It would seem that Galtung is correct in his view of North-South structures, but he and other structuralists are less than accurate when discussing the precise impacts of the international system on developing nations. In reference to the first alleged effect, that of cultural imperialism, one finds that increases in economic development, not increased Western media imports, are associated with westernization. Therefore, economic growth, industrialization, and urbanization are greater cultural threats to most LDCs than is Western media fare.

Pertaining to the second alleged effect, that of Western media promoting endemic unrest, we once again have a non-finding. Endemic violence of the sort quantified in this study increases along with economic development, but endemic violence is not associated with Western media imported. There can be little doubt that the herd mentality, sensationalism, and globe-skipping nature of Western journalism act to promote some types of episodic violence (e.g., terrorism). Episodes of terrorism are an increasing problem (Joint Chiefs of Staff, 1987: 91), but a problem primarily for those Western powers most frequently targeted. Endemic violence is the greater problem for the Third World. Endemic violence, by its very nature, is a daily problem. Its effects are experienced more frequently by LDCs than are the effects of episodic violence, and endemic violence is experienced more frequently by LDCs than by the states of the West.

Let us be clear on what is *not* being said here. I am not saying that Western media are unrelated to episodic violence in LDCs (or in advanced industrialized states, for that matter). In fact, a proper understanding of

Western news as a commodity reveals that the opposite is true. Western media seek out the sensational. Terrorists and national liberation fronts play to this tendency of the free press for their own gain. Both sides know what sells.

Of course, as with any approach, the methods used here to address these issues have their limits. Other measures of westernization and endemic violence could be postulated. The serial nature of the tests was designed with this limitation in mind. Test results have identified the neocolonial structure of international communication. With regard to the causal links between Western media and either cultural imperialism or endemic violence, however, we are left with non-findings. But even these non-findings can tell us a great deal. No matter how the tests were run, the results were consistent. Regardless of which of the many areas of westernization the tests focused on, and even when endemic violence was measured via very different indices that are negatively correlated with one another, the findings remained consistent between the predictors and the dependent variables. The most striking of these consistencies is that there is no relationship between Western media and either westernization or endemic violence in the Third World.

These tests were not designed to "falsify" Galtung's theory of structuralism. To show that a theory has holes in its intellectual fabric is insufficient proof to justify dismissing that theory in toto. Galtung's depiction of North-South interactions remains unrefuted. Therefore, any accurate international relations (IR) theory must, in the future, incorporate some of the essential elements of structural thought. IR theory in the late twentieth century (e.g., Waltz's systemic theory) is necessarily incomplete if it neglects such elements of the global system as Center-Periphery interactions and domination or dependency. By contrast, Galtung's work, like dependency theory, is "correct in focusing on structural conditions" that govern the political economy of North-South relations (Clark, 1987: 327).

Testing structural thought is a necessary condition, but not a sufficient condition for advancing IR theory. True scientific advancement comes about only when *alternatives* to a prior and incomplete understanding of the world have been offered (Bueno de Mesquita, 1985). This study does not falsify structuralism because, in order to truly falsify any position, one must be able to offer "a demonstrably superior understanding of the world" (Bueno de Mesquita, 1985: 122). Following Bueno de Mesquita, one should seek to refute established theories only if the ultimate goal is what Lakatos termed "sophisticated methodological falsification" (1985: 123). One may reject the validity of structuralism only when an alternative theory has been developed that accounts for the reality of global politics that structuralism seems best able to describe. No grand theory of this type will be presented here, nor is any in the offing from the mainstream of IR literature.

Table 6.1:
A Typology of Economic Development and Press Freedom

		ECONOMIC DEVELOPMENT	
		High	Low
PRESS FREEDOM	High	Group A	Group B
	Low	Group C	Group D

Table 6.2:
LDC Rankings According to Sovereignty and Stability

	CULTURAL SOVEREIGNTY	POLITICAL STABILITY
ORDINAL RANKINGS	1) Group D 2) Group C 3) Group B 4) Group A	1) Group B 2) Group A 3) Group D 4) Group C

How might structuralism progress, given its relative strengths and weaknesses? Suggestions for theoretical refinement and further research will follow a final consideration of public policy in the area of communication.

LDC ECONOMIES AND PRESS FREEDOM LEVELS: SOVEREIGNTY VERSUS STABILITY

Economic development and press freedom are the most powerful explanatory variables in this study in terms of their ability to account for westernization and political instability in developing nations. Indicators of media imports add little or no explanatory power to the tests, despite structural theories to the contrary. By combining what we have learned from the numerous empirical tests, one can create a fourfold typology that divides LDCs according to levels of development and media regulation (see Table 6.1). Having created these categories analytically, the likely trends for each group of nations in the areas of westernization and political instability—given the results of this study—are easily derived (see Table 6.2).

Developing nations in Group A would include those such as Argentina and Singapore that have relatively high levels of both economic development and press freedom (i.e., GNP per capita greater than $2,000; press freedom rankings above the mean value of .30). As one can see from Table 6.2, these nations are the most vulnerable to Western enculturation, but they also rank well (second as a group) in terms of political stability. Higher levels of economic output and press freedom combine to endanger the indigenous ways of life in Group A nations; however, an unrestricted media would, at the same time, tend to promote greater political tolerance and less unrest.

Group B nations also have above average levels of press freedom, but are less fortunate in terms of their national wealth (e.g., Colombia, India). Westernization is less of a threat to these nations, as compared with countries in Group A, because of their lower levels of development. In spite of this fact, the presence of press freedom indicates that this group of nations would rank low (third) on the scale of cultural sovereignty. On the other hand, these are the nations which, on the whole, would tend to have the stablest societies—with widespread press freedom and lower levels of wealth combining to dampen the heat of political tensions. These factors might help to explain, for example, the relative stability of India's democracy (Group B), as compared with the oscillation between democracy and "bureaucratic-authoritarianism" in Argentina (Group A).

Nations in Group C (e.g., Iran, Iraq) have higher levels of economic output, but below average values for press freedom. These nations would tend to rank high (second) as a group in measures of cultural independence (an independence displayed forcefully by the Ayatollah Khomeini's fundamentalist and anti-Western revolution), but would also tend to rank low (last as a group) in political stability. Higher levels of development tend to be associated with socio-political violence, while the absence of press freedom removes a principal means for defusing that violence.

Those nations in the final group, Group D, would tend to be the least westernized due to the combination of low economic growth and lack of press freedom. However, these countries are in the unenviable position of being not only poor, but also relatively unstable (again due to an absence of press freedom—nations from the sample in this group would include Ethiopia and Jordan).

Clearly there is a trade-off that must be considered when discussing the effects of media policies on developing nations. If one can assume that few LDCs would willingly opt for a low level of economic development simply to avoid Western cultural influences or instability (although the Islamic fundamentalism of Khomeini seems to be very close to this stance), then a key lesson to which much of my research points is this: press freedom can provide real benefits to LDCs, but as they gain something they also lose something. As Third World nations tend to become politically stabler with increasing levels of press freedom, by the same token they also place themselves in greater risk of adopting Western cultural traits.

Leadership of a developing nation is often an exercise in the making of hard choices, while working under constraints imposed by limited natural resources and the extant structure of international relations (Rothstein, 1977). Setting media policy does not differ significantly in this regard from setting policy for industrialization or urban growth. Difficult choices must be made and trade-offs between goals (e.g, whether to stress cultural sovereignty or political stability) must be faced squarely. It is hoped that the research which has been presented here has provided the new data and new analyses required to assist policymakers in the Third World in addressing these onerous tasks.

LIKELY CRITIQUES OF THIS STUDY FROM A STRUCTURAL OR *DEPENDENCIA* PERSPECTIVE

This research has studied communication primarily at the national level.[2] This has not been a comparative study of particular communication policies at the subnational level. Chapters Four and Five looked for broad trends and associations that hold across the Third World as a whole. Structural and *dependencia* theorists often fault research at this level for not taking into account more of the culture-specific variables that exist in the numerous Third World nations.

A classic work of *dependencia* theory—Cardoso and Faletto's *Dependency and Development in Latin America*—criticizes prior studies of dependency on just these grounds. They see

little sense in attempting to measure "degrees of dependency" [and] making formal comparisons of dependent situations.... The rationale behind such a methodology is based on the possible common effect of a general (thus for us "abstract") form of dependency that permeates all types of situations. (1979: xii)

Cardoso and Faletto deride quantitative techniques of the type employed here because "the methodological status of measurement in a dialectical approach does not play the role of a fundamental device in the logic of demonstration, as if we were dealing with hypotheses to be accepted or rejected only after statistical tests." It is this "dialectical approach" which these authors prefer to quantitative methods. They claim that theirs is a methodology which "require[s] an effort to specify each new situation in the search for differences and diversity" (1979: xii-xiii).

The same critique, I trust, would be leveled at this study. Admittedly, the "differences and diversity" of each of the twenty-four nations in my sample have not been fully specified here. To put this criticism into slightly different terminology, *dependencia* theorists prefer relativist or idiographic research to that which is generalist or nomothetic (see Przeworski and Teune, 1970: 5–13).

The fact remains, however, that if structural and *dependencia* claims regarding international communication are to retain any intelligibility, then certain general propositions must hold true. If increased inputs of Western media lead to a demonstration effect which stimulates cultural imperialism, then those nations with higher levels of imported media must, as a group, at least tend to be more westernized in their socio-economic systems than nations with lower levels of imported media. It is difficult to see what else structural theory could imply. This is the logic that underlies the empirical tests of this study, tests based on structural and dependency theories as they now stand. Test results show that many of the relationships which these theories predict simply do not hold.

LEVELS OF ANALYSIS AND WHERE DO WE GO FROM HERE?

Although this research has not produced support for most structural claims, neither does it refute structural theory of international communication once and for all. The way these tests have been conducted does partake in some ways of the form of "critical" tests favored by some logical-empiricist philosophies of science (e.g., Popper's falsification thesis). But these tests are not intended to be the final word on the subject. Rather, certain central points of contention in a current policy debate have been put into a theoretical context and then tested. It is hoped that, rather than close off or end the policy debate, the theoretically guided research discussed here will produce hard evidence that can lead to renewed discussions on specific points. These policy debates currently tend to stay at the ideological-abstract level, a trend which promises to end all hope of fruitful discussions (due to the withdrawl of the United States from Unesco because that body is said to have become too "politicized").

One should not expect structural theorists to abandon their positions, given the results of this study. The strongly felt political commitments which underlie their theoretical postures make this a highly unlikely occurrence. However, it is hoped that the results presented here will induce some structuralists to go back to the drawing board and refine their theories. This study has shown that when certain arguments from structural theory of international communication are empirically tested, the results tend to refute several of their central points. On the other hand, this research could even be seen as providing them with the first steps in the right direction toward refining their own thought.

Most of the research of this study has been conducted at the national level, but it also has pointed to certain subnational factors that should be taken into account in future studies regarding international communication and Third World development. For example:

1. Results from Chapter Four suggested that developing nations can be divided into two groups: those which have high levels of press freedom and economic westernization versus those which have low levels of both of these factors. A preliminary suggestion was then made to control for regime type, and see if this move helps to explain the differences in media policies for these two groups.
2. Results from the same chapter also showed evidence of LDCs adopting a strategy of import substitution industry (ISI: continued importation of capital and industrial goods while building local industries to produce consumer goods). As press freedom increased, absolute expenditures on luxury goods increased while, at the same time, consumer goods as a percentage of all imports dropped. This is a trend one would expect to find in nations which pursue ISI strategies. Incorporating an indicator of nations which do/do not pursue ISI may help to account for this particular aspect of the relationship between media policies and economic development in the Third World.

These points illustrate the utility of higher-level analyses in pointing out directions for subsequent case studies. It would seem that, despite *dependencia* claims to the contrary, study at the higher national level has uncovered variables at the subnational level which ought to be pursued through further analysis. Just which nations fall into the two groups in points 1 or 2 above would probably require more in-depth case studies. A third possibility for case studies would be to look at examples in which "relevance" was taken into consideration when making LDC communication policy (e.g., by incorporating modern technologies and traditional modes of communication) and comparing the successes and failures of this approach.

Note that the particular types of cases that have been identified—those in which more thoroughly "idiographic" studies would hold the most promise—are cases that have been revealed through the somewhat "nomothetic" studies of this book. Case studies, then, could be seen as a useful complement to studies like this one at the national level, and vice versa. Studies at both levels could help to refine one another.

The general heuristic implication of this argument is that moving from one level of analysis to another, and back again, is a process which can increase the theoretical sophistication of work at each level. This investigation could be viewed, in one respect, as an example of the first step in such a process. It has shown that further study is needed, what level of analysis that research might be conducted at, and what the next steps at that level could be.

NOTES

1. *Dependencia* (dependency) theory is closely related to structural theory in its analysis of international relations. Both theories describe a condition of dependent, exploitive relations between the West and the Third World. Both see the sources of most problems of national development in LDCs in the political and economic foreign policies of advanced industrialized nations. These theories also share many of the same policy proposals. Because the two schools of thought are so closely related when it comes to their treatments of international relations, I will address both groups (and their likely criticisms of my research) in this concluding chapter. For examples of areas in which structural and *dependencia* theory overlap, see the introduction and the discussion of the demonstration effect in Chapter Four, and the discussion of the ideology of news as a social good in Chapter Two.

2. This is true of Chapters Four and Five and the analysis of aggregate data in Chapter Three. The one exception to this assertion would be the news flow study of African dailies.

Bibliography

Aggarwala, Narinda (1979). "What Is Development News?" *Journal of Communication* 29 (2): 115–126.
Alexander, Jeffery C. (1981). "The Mass Media in Systemic, Historical, and Comparative Perspective." In Katz and Szecsko: 17–52.
Alker, Hayward R. (1966). "Causal Inferences and Political Analysis." In Joseph Bernd (ed.), *Mathematical Applications in Political Science*. Dallas: Southern Methodist University Press.
Altheide, David L. (1987). "Format and Coverage of Terrorism in the United States and Great Britain." *International Studies Quarterly* 31 (2): 161–167.
Altheide, David L., and John M. Johnson (1980). *Bureaucratic Propaganda*. Boston: Allyn and Bacon.
Apter, David E. (1965). *The Politics of Modernization*. Chicago: University of Chicago Press.
Baer, Werner (1972). "Import Substitution and Industrialization in Latin America." *Quarterly Journal of Economics* 7 (1): 95–122.
Becker, Jiorg, Gioran Hedebro, and Leena Paldian (eds.) (1986). *Communication and Domination: Essays to Honor Herbert I. Schiller*. Norwood, N.J.: Ablex-Norwood.
Beitz, Charles R. (1979). *Political Theory and International Relations*. Princeton, N.J.: Princeton University Press.
Bennett, W. Lance (1983). *News: The Politics of Illusion*. New York: Longman.
Bhattacharya, Vivek Ranjan (1976). *Communication in a Global Village*. New Delhi: Chetana.
Blake, Cecil (1979). "Communications Research and African National Development." *Journal of Black Studies* 10 (2): 218–230.
Bueno de Mesquita, Bruce (1985). "Toward a Scientific Understanding of International Conflict: A Personal View." *International Studies Quarterly* 29 (2): 121–136.
Burnet, Mary (1971). *The Mass Media in a Violent World*. Paris: Unesco.

Cardoso, Fernando Henrique, and Enzo Faletto (1979). *Dependency and Development in Latin America*. Berkeley: University of California Press.

Carpini, M. X. D. and B. A. Williams (1987). "Television and Terrorism—Patterns of Presentation and Occurrence, 1969 to 1980." *Western Political Quarterly* 40 (1): 45–64.

Chaney, David (1981). "Public Opinion and Social Change: The Social Rhetoric of Documentary and the Concept of News." In Katz and Szecsko: 115–136.

Cioffi-Revilla, Claudio, Richard Merritt, and Dina A. Zinnes (eds.) (1987). *Communication and Interaction in Global Politics*. Beverly Hills, Calif.: Sage.

Clark, Cal (1987). "The Taiwan Exception: Implications for Contending Political Economy Paradigms." *International Studies Quarterly* 31 (3): 327–356.

Coate, Roger A. (1988). *Multilateralism at Bay: The United States In and Out of UNESCO*. Boulder, Colo.: Lynne Rienner.

Cox, Robert W. (1986). "Social Forces, States and World Orders: Beyond International Relations Theory." In Robert O. Keohane (ed.), *Neorealism and Its Critics*. New York: Columbia University Press.

d'Arcy, Jean (1981). "The Right to Communicate." In Richstad and Anderson: 117–136.

Davison, W. Phillips (1965). *International Political Communication*. New York: Praeger.

Desmond, Robert W. (1978). *The Information Process: World News Reporting to the Twentieth Century*. Iowa City: University of Iowa Press.

——— (1980). *Windows on the World: World News Reporting 1900–1920*. Iowa City: University of Iowa Press.

——— (1982). *Crisis and Conflict: World News Reporting Between Two Wars 1920–1940*. Iowa City: University of Iowa Press.

Deutsch, Karl W. (1961). "Social Mobilization and Political Development." *American Political Science Review* 55 (September): 493–514.

Dougherty, James E., and Robert L. Pfaltzgraff (1981). *Contending Theories of International Relations*. New York: Harper and Row.

Frenkel, Roberto, and Guillermo O'Donnell (1979). "The Stabilization Programs of the International Monetary Fund and Their Internal Impacts." In Richard R. Fagen (ed.), *Capitalism and the State in U.S.-Latin American Relations*. Stanford: Stanford University Press.

Frey, Frederick W. (1973). "Communication and Development." In Ithiel de Sola Pool, Frederick W. Frey, et al. (eds.), *Handbook of Communication*. Chicago: Rand McNally.

Friedman, Milton (1973). *Money and Economic Development*. New York: Praeger.

Galtung, Johan (1979). "A Structural Theory of Imperialism." In George Modelski (ed.), *Transnational Corporations and World Order*. San Francisco: W. H. Freeman.

——— (1980). *The True Worlds*. New York: The Free Press.

Giffard, C. Anthony (1985). "The Inter Press Service: New Information for a New Order." *Journalism Quarterly* 62 (1): 17–23.

Gilpin, Robert (1981). *War and Change in World Politics*. New York: Cambridge University Press.

Golding, Peter (1981). "The Missing Dimension—News Media and the Management of Social Change." In Katz and Szecsko: 63–82.

Goodman, Jay S. (1965). "The Concept of 'System' in International Relations Theory." *Background* 8 (4): 257–268.
Halloran, James D. (1980). "Mass Communication: Symptom or Cause of Violence?" In G. Cleveland Wilhoit and Harold de Bock, *Mass Communication Review Yearbook, vol. I*. Beverly Hills, Calif.: Sage.
Harris, Phil (1981a). *Reporting Southern Africa*. Paris: Unesco.
——— (1981b). "News Dependence and Structural Change." In Richstad and Anderson: 365–368.
Harris, Phil, Harald Malczek and Etrugrul Ozkok (1982). "Flow of News in the Gulf." *Documents on the New Communication Order #3*. New York: UniPub.
Haynes, Robert D., Jr. (1984). "Test of Galtung's Theory of Structural Imperialism." In Stevenson and Shaw: 200–216.
Hirschman, Albert O. (1968). "The Political Economy of Import-Substituting Industrialization in Latin America." *Quarterly Journal of Economics* 82 (1): 1–30.
Hornik, R. C. (1975). "Mass Media and the Revolution of Rising Expectations: A Reconsideration of the Theory." *Papers of the East-West Institute* (Honolulu), no. 11.
Huntington, Samuel P. (1968). *Political Order in Changing Societies*. New Haven, Conn.: Yale University Press.
International Press Institute (1953). *The Flow of News*. Zurich: I.P.I.
Jacobson, Harold K. (1984). "U.S. Withdrawal from UNESCO: Incident, Warning or Prelude?" *PS* 17 (3): 581–585.
Joint Chiefs of Staff (1987). *Military Posture, FY 1987*. Washington, D.C.: Government Printing Office.
Joyner, Christopher C., and Scott A. Lawson (1985–1986). "The United States and UNESCO: Rethinking the Decision to Withdraw." *International Journal* 41 (Winter): 37–71.
Kaplan, Morton A. (1975). *System and Process in International Politics*. Huntington, N.Y.: Kreiger.
Katz, Elihu, and Tamas Szecsko (eds.) (1981). *Mass Media and Social Change*. Beverly Hills, Calif.: Sage.
Katz, Elihu, and George Wedell (1977). *Broadcasting in the Third World: Promise and Performance*. Cambridge, Mass.: Harvard University Press.
Krasner, Stephen D. (1985). *Structural Conflict: The Third World Against Global Liberalism*. Berkeley: University of California Press.
Kurian, George Thomas (1979). *The Book of World Rankings*. New York: Facts on File.
——— (1982). *World Press Encyclopedia*. New York: Facts on File.
——— (1984). *The New Book of World Rankings*. New York: Facts on File.
Lanigan, Richard L., and Rudolf L. Strobl (1981). "A Critical Theory Approach." In Nimmo and Sanders: 142–150.
Lerner, Daniel (1964). *The Passing of Traditional Society: Modernizing the Middle East*. New York: The Free Press.
Link, Jere H. (1984). "Test of the Cultural Dependency Hypothesis." In Stevenson and Shaw: 186–199.

MacBride Commission (1981a). "Communication Problems Today." In Richstad and Anderson: 35–55.
——— (1981b). "Communication Tomorrow." In Richstad and Anderson: 380–401.
Martin, L. John (1983). "Africa." In John C. Merrill (ed.), *Global Journalism*. New York: Longman.
Martz, John D. (ed.) (1971). *The Dynamics of Change in Latin American Politics*. Englewood Cliffs, N.J.: Prentice-Hall.
Marx, Karl. *Das Kapital: A Critique of Political Economy*. Chicago: Regnery Gateway.
Masmoudi, Mustapha (1979). "The New World Information Order." *Journal of Communication* 29 (2): 172–185.
——— (1981). "The New World Information Order." In Richstad and Anderson: 77–98.
McCrone, Donald J., and Charles F. Cnudde (1967). "Toward a Communications Theory of Democratic Political Development: A Causal Model." *American Political Science Review* 61 (March): 72–79.
McPhail, Thomas (1987). *Electronic Colonialism: The Future of International Broadcasting and Communication*. Beverly Hills, Calif.: Sage.
Merrill, John C. (1981). "A Growing Controversy: The 'Free Flow' of News." In Richstad and Anderson: 151–160.
Meyer, William H. (1984). "The Concept of 'News' and Processes of Social Change." *Occasional Papers, Report #11*. Iowa City: Laboratory for Political Research.
——— (1985). "Western Versus Third World Journalistic Practice." Paper presented at the Annual Meeting of the Midwest Political Science Association.
——— (1987). "Testing Theories of Cultural Imperialism." *International Interactions* 13 (4): 353–374.
——— (1988). "International Information Flows as a Determinant of Political Violence in Third World Nations: Fact or Fiction?" *Social Science Quarterly* 69 (1): 24–39.
Mowlana, Hamid (1986). *Global Information and World Communication: New Frontiers in International Relations*. New York: Longman.
Nimmo, Dan D., and Keith R. Sanders (1981). *Handbook of Political Communication*. Norwood, N.J.: Ablex.
O'Brien, Rita Cruise, and G. K. Helleniner, (1980). "The Political Economy of Information in a Changing International Economic Order." *International Organization* 34 (4): 445–470.
O'Donnell, Guillermo (1973). *Modernization and Bureaucratic-Authoritarianism*. Berkeley, Calif.: Institute of International Studies.
Oxford English Dictionary (1970). Oxford: Clarendon Press.
Pinch, Edward T. (1978). "A Brief Study of News Patterns in Sixteen Third World Countries." *Occasional Papers*. Medford, Mass.: Edward R. Murrow Center of Public Diplomacy, Tufts University.
Przeworski, Adam, and Henry Teune (1970). *The Logic of Comparative Social Inquiry*. New York: John Wiley and Sons.
Richstad, Jim, and Michael A. Anderson (eds.) (1981). *Crisis in International News: Policies and Prospects*. New York: Columbia University Press.

Righter, Rosemary (1978). *Whose News? Politics, the Press, and the Third World.* New York: Time Books.
——— (1981). "World Communication Issues." In Richstad and Anderson: 56–76.
Rogers, Everett M., and Jorge Reina Schement (eds.) (1984). *Media Flows in Latin America.* Beverly Hills, Calif.: Sage.
Roser, Connie, and Lee Brown (1986). "African Newspaper Editors and the New World Information Order." *Journalism Quarterly* 63 (1): 114–121.
Rothstein, Robert L. (1977). *The Weak in the World of the Strong.* New York: Columbia University Press.
Schiller, Herbert I. (1976). *Communication and Cultural Domination.* White Plains, N.Y.: M. E. Sharpe.
——— (1981). "Genesis of the Free Flow of Information Principles." In Richstad and Anderson: 161–183.
Schmid, Alex P., and Janny deGraff (1982). *Violence as Communication.* Beverly Hills, Calif.: Sage.
Schramm, Wilbur L. (1964). *Mass Media and National Development.* Stanford, Calif.: Stanford University Press.
——— (1980). "Circulation of News in the Third World: A Study of Asia." In G. Cleveland Wilhoit and Harold de Bock (eds.), *Mass Communication Review Yearbook*: 589–619. Beverly Hills, Calif.: Sage.
——— (1981). "International News Wires and Third World News in Asia." In Richstad and Anderson: 197–218.
Schramm, Wilbur L., and Erwin Atwood (1981). *Circulation of News in the Third World: A Study of Asia.* Hong Kong: Chinese University Press.
Sidel, M. Kent (1984). "The New World Information Order in Action in Guyana." *Journalism Quarterly* 61 (3): 493–498.
Siebert, Fred S. (1956). "The Libertarian Theory." In Fred S. Siebert, Theodore Peterson, and Wilbur Schramm (eds.), *Four Theories of the Press.* Urbana: University of Illinois Press.
Smith, Anthony (1980). *The Geopolitics of Information: How Western Culture Dominates the World.* New York: Oxford University Press.
Sommerlad, E. Lloyd (1975). "National Communication Systems: Some Policy Issues and Options." *Reports and Papers on Mass Communication #74.* New York: Unesco.
Spero, Joan Edelman (1982). "Information, the Policy Void." *Foreign Policy* 48: 139–156.
Stevenson, Robert L. (1981). "Beyond Belgrade: Prospects for a Balanced Flow of Information." Paper presented to the International Studies Association.
Stevenson, Robert L., and Richard R. Cole (1980). "Patterns of World Coverage by the Major Western Agencies." Paper presented to the Inter-Cultural Communication Division, International Communication Association.
Stevenson, Robert L. and Donald Lewis Shaw (eds.) (1984). *Foreign News and the New World Information Order.* Ames, Ia.: Iowa State University Press.
Sussman, Leonard R. (ed.) (1981a). *Freedom in the World*, 1980. New York: Freedom House.
——— (1981b). "Western Media and the Third World's Challenge." In Richstad and Anderson: 344–355.

Taylor, Charles Lewis, and David A. Jodice (eds.) (1983). *World Handbook of Political and Social Indicators*. New Haven, Conn.: Yale University Press.

Tuchman, Gaye (1981). "Myth and the Consciousness Industry: A New Look at the Effects of Mass Media." In Katz and Szecsko: 83–100.

Tufte, Edward R. (1974). *Data Analysis for Politics and Policy*. Englewood Cliffs, N.J.: Prentice-Hall.

Unesco (1980). *Many Voices, One World*. New York: UniPub.

U.S. Department of State (October, 1981). *Department of State Bulletin*. Washington, D.C.: U.S. Department of State.

────── (June, 1982). *Department of State Bulletin*. Washington, D.C.: U.S. Department of State.

Waltz, Kenneth N. (1979). *Theory of International Relations*. New York: Random House.

Weston, Burns H., Richard A. Falk, and Anthony A. D'Amato (eds.) (1980). *Basic Documents in International Law and World Order*. St. Paul, Minn.: West.

Wills, Gary (1979). *Nixon Agonistes: The Crisis of the Self-made Man*. New York: New American Library.

Index

Abel, Elie, 7, 91 n.1
Advertising, 8, 14, 92 n.13; as an indicator of westernization, 70–72, 74–81, 86–88; relation to a free press, 76; violence and, 98–100
Africa, 2, 14, 28, 39 nn.1, 5, 42, 44–51, 56–58, 61 n.4, 73, 88 98, 111–12, 121 n.2
Agence France Press (AFP), 5, 21–22, 36, 51–52, 56, 60, 66, 112; coverage within former French colonies, 56–57
Alexander, Jeffery, 22
Alker, Hayward, 38
Altheide, David, 25, 96
Anderson, Michael, 2, 6, 8, 10, 17, 91 n.1, 95. *See also* Richstad, Jim
Apter, David, 76, 101
Argentina, 73, 92 n.8, 93 n.16, 93 n.20, 117
ASEAN, 17
Asia, 22, 45, 47–51, 73, 88, 98, 107
Associated Press (AP), 5, 20–22, 36, 50–52, 56–57, 60, 66, 112; coverage within U.S. hegemonic sphere, 56–57; evolution of, 20–22
Australia, 22

Beitz, Charles, 26
Belgium, 44

Belgrade, 6
Bennett, W. Lance, 25, 33
Big Four, 21, 36, 47–48, 50–52, 58–59, 112
Blake, Cecil, 41–42
Britain, 18, 44; British Empire, 22, 56–58
Broadcasting, 4, 14, 28, 41, 47, 58, 64, 69, 72, 74, 76, 78–79, 84–85, 88–89, 91 n.4, 95, 97, 101; satellites and, 32, 35, 39 n.4, 65; in the Third World, 42–43
Bueno de Mesquita, Bruce, 115
Buenos Aires, 33, 44
Bureaucratized media, 24–25, 32
Burnet, Mary, 96–98, 100–101, 107

Cardoso, Fernando, 55, 111, 118–19; *Dependency and Development in Latin America*, 118
Censorship, 8, 91 n.5
Chile, 60 n.2, 73, 92 n.8, 93 n.16
China, 22
Cnudde, Charles, 38
Coate, Roger, 2
Cole, Richard, 44, 49, 58
Colombia, 73, 93 n.20, 117
Communication and development: Lerner Thesis, 34–37; Structural

Thesis, 36–39, 65–68, 74–91, 112; theories of, 11–12, 33–37
Cultural imperialism, 3, 10, 12–13, 15, 59, 64, 86–91, 98, 112–15, 119; cultural sovereignty and development, 116–18; measures of, 69–72; theories of, 10, 65–69; in the Third and Fourth Worlds, 79–81, 90–91

Daily Nation, 43–44, 46, 48, 60, 61 n.5
Democratized media, 11, 31–33
Demonstration effect, 3, 14, 37, 42, 44, 64–65, 71–72, 87–89, 98, 108, 112, 119, 121 n.1
Dependency theory. *See* Cardoso, Fernando
de Sola Pool, Ithiel, 25
Deutsch, Karl, 35
Development. *See* Communication and development
Developmental journalism. *See* Journalism.
Direct broadcast satellite (DBS). *See* Broadcasting.
Dollard, John, 99
Dougherty, James, 99

Egypt, 22, 61 n.8, 73, 93 n.19
Ethiopia, 60 n.2, 73, 93 n.19, 117
Europe, 20, 22, 48, 65
Excelsior, 43–44, 48, 60

Faletto, Enzo, 55, 111, 118–19; *Dependency and Development in Latin America*, 118
France, 19, 44, 56–57, 60, 79
Freedom House, 6
Free flow of information, 8–9, 23, 26, 34, 36, 38, 60, 90, 101, 107
Free press, 7–9, 26, 29–32, 63, 67, 74, 98, 115
Frey, Frederick, 34–35, 38

Galtung, Johan, 13, 15, 36, 42, 45, 51, 55–56, 59, 71, 81, 88, 111, 113–15; as structuralist, 10
Germany, 19, 44

Ghana, 60 n.2, 73, 93 n.19
Golding, Peter, 23–24

Habermas, Jurgen, 31
Halloran, James, 96–100
Harris, Phil, 10, 44–45, 51, 65, 67–68
Haynes, Robert, 55–57
Helleiner, G. K., 2
Huntington, Samuel, 35

Import substitution industry (ISI), 85, 120. *See also* Prebisch, Raul
India, 22, 30, 39 n.4, 60 n.2, 73, 117
International Press Institute (IPI), 44
International Program for the Development of Communication (IPDC), 6
Inter-Press Service (IPS), 28, 51
Iran, 2, 60 n.2, 73, 93 nn.16, 19, 117
Iraq, 60 n.2, 73, 92 n.8, 93 nn.16, 19, 117

Jamaica, 60 n.2, 73, 93 n.20
Japan, 22, 65
Jefferson, Thomas, 34
Jodice, David, 103, 105, 109 n.4, 110 nn.7, 9
Jordan, 60 n.2, 73, 92 n.8, 93 n.19, 117
Journalism: developmental style, 28–30; Leninist, 30–31; liberal theory of, 34; objectivity, 20–21

Kaplan, Morton, 114
Katz, Elihu, 79–80, 82, 97
Kenya, 17, 30, 39 n.1, 43, 51, 56
Kurian, George, 44, 72, 74, 91 n.5, 103, 105, 110 n.8

Lakatos, Imre, 115
La Nacion, 44, 48, 60
La Prensa, 44, 48, 60
Latin America, 20, 22, 42–43, 45, 47–51, 55, 57–59, 61 n.5, 73, 111
Latin American Institute for Transnational Studies (ILET), 29–30
Lebanon, 73, 92 n.8, 93 n.20
Lerner, Daniel, 7, 11, 25, 34–39, 76,

101; *The Passing of Traditional Society*, 34. *See also* Communication and development.
Liberalism, 26
London, 19
Los Angeles Times, 47

MacBride, Sean, 8
MacBride Commission, 1–2, 5–6, 8–11, 30, 39 n.3; Final Report, 1, 6–7; Interim Report, 1
Marcuse, Herbert, 36
Marx, Karl, 21, 36

Masmoudi, Mustafa, 5, 29, 31–32, 51, 64, 68
Mass media, 7, 9, 12, 15, 17, 23, 33, 35–36, 38, 41, 63–64, 66, 96–98, 101–2, 107–8
McCronne, Donald, 38
McPhail, Thomas, 2, 6, 14, 43–44, 64, 68, 70, 98
Merril, John, 7, 58
Mexico, 73, 92 n.8, 93 n.20
Mexico City, 44
Middle East, 7, 22, 48, 73
Mill, John Stuart, 34, 101
Mody, Bella, 39 n.4
Morocco, 73
Multinational corporation (MNC), 4–5, 26, 56, 65

Nairobi, 43, 46
New International Economic Order (NIEO), 1, 10, 74; platform, 4; program of implementation, 6; relation to NWIO, 5–6
News: as a commodity, 18–23; developmental, 28–29, 46, 49, 52–54; international flows of, 55–58, 60; lead/body format, 20–21; sensationalism, 19–20; as a social good, 27–29; spot reports of crises, 45–46, 49, 52–53. *See also* Journalism.
Newswires, 7–8, 49, 51–55, 58, 74
New World Information Order (NWIO), 1–2, 4, 9–10, 16 n.1, 17, 24, 26–27, 29–33, 42, 47, 51, 56, 61 n.3, 63–64, 67, 69, 74, 98, 101, 108, 111, 113; platform, 5; program of implementation, 6; relation to NIEO, 5–6
New York Times, 47
Nigeria, 60 n.2, 73, 92 n.8, 93 n.19, 97
Nonaligned News Pool (Tanjung), 28, 32

O'Brien, Rita Cruise, 2
O'Donnell, Guillermo, 85
OPEC, 4
Organization for Economic Cooperation and Development (OECD), 15, 17

Pakistan, 60 n.2, 73, 93 n.19
Panama, 60 n.2, 73, 92 n.8, 93 n.20
Pfaltzgraff, Robert, 99
Pinch, Edward, 47, 49
Popper, Sir Karl, 119
Portugal, 44
Prebisch, Raul, 85
Programme of Action, 6. *See also* New International Economic Order (NIEO)
Propaganda, 25, 63, 98
Pye, Lucien, 25

Radio, 5, 35, 41–43, 58, 60 n.2, 64, 97
Reagan Administration, 1–2, 63; policy on the NWIO, 2; withdrawal from Unesco, 63
Reuter, Paul Julius, 19. *See also* Reuters news service
Reuters news service, 5, 13, 36, 44, 50–52, 56, 58, 60, 66, 112; clientele, 19–20; control of communication technology, 22–23; coverage of events in former British colonies, 56–57; early years, 19–21; prewar news monopoly, 22–23
Richstad, Jim, 2, 6, 8, 17, 91 n.1, 95
Righter, Rosemary, 17–18, 21, 28, 30, 39 nn.2, 3
Right to communicate, 9, 33
Ring Combination: creation of, 22; current legacy, 58–59; end of, 22

Schiller, Herbert, 10–11, 23–24, 36–37, 42, 64, 67–68, 70–72, 81, 88, 111, 113; policy recommendations, 11, 37, 70–71; as a structuralist, 10. *See also* Structuralism

Schramm, Wilbur, 38, 43–44, 112; news flow study of Asia, 45, 47–51

Senegal, 60 n.2, 97

Siebert, Fred, 30

Singapore, 60 n.2, 73, 92 n.8, 93 nn.16, 20, 117

Smith, Anthony, 18–20, 25, 28–30, 39 n.2, 64

Somavia, Juan, 29–30, 39 n.3

Sommerlad, E. Lloyd, 5

South Korea, 60 n.2, 73

Special Service, Reuter's, 19–20

Spero, Joan, 8

Spheres of influence, informational, 3, 44, 57–58, 60

Spot news. *See* News.

Sri Lanka, 60 n.2, 73

Standard operating procedure (SOP), 24–25

Stevenson, Robert, 44, 49, 58–59

Structuralism, 9–11, 36–39, 65–66, 87–90, 111–15; characterization of international news flows, 42, 55–56; theorists of, 9–11

Sussman, Leonard, 6–7, 24, 32

Syria, 60 n.2, 73, 93 n.19

Szecsko, Tamas, 23

Tanzania, 46, 97

TASS, 31

Taylor, Charles Lewis, 103, 105, 109 n.4, 110 nn.7, 9

Technology, communication, 4–5, 7, 10, 19, 22, 28, 35, 37, 39 n.4

Television, 5, 35, 41–43, 58, 60 n.2, 64, 97, 111

Terrorism: as a form of episodic violence, 97; news coverage of, 96–97, 114–15

Times of Zambia, 43–44, 46, 48, 60, 61 nn.5, 6

Transnational news agencies (TNNAs). *See* Agence France Press (AFP), Associate Press (AP), Reuters news service, United Press International (UPI)

Tufte, Edward, 78

Tuluhungwa, Revi, 37, 39 n.5, 41

Tunisia, 5, 30–31, 60 n.2

Unesco, 1–2, 5–6, 9, 15, 33, 42–43, 60 n.1, 61 n.3, 63–64, 69, 72, 74–75, 82, 91 nn.4, 7, 92 n.12, 95–96, 98, 100, 103, 107–8, 111–12, 119; promotion of the NWIO, 5–6; reaction to U.S. withdrawal, 63. *See also* MacBride Commission

United Kingdom, 56, 61 n.8, 79

United Nations, 1, 4, 6, 72, 84–85

United Press International (UPI), 5, 21–22, 36, 50–52, 56–57, 60, 66, 112; coverage within U.S. hegemonic sphere, 56–57; evolution of, 21

United States, 2, 7–8, 15, 18–21, 48, 56, 91 n.3, 119; withdrawal from Unesco, 63

Uruguay, 73, 93

Varis, Tapio, 91 n.4

Violence, 20, 32, 95, 112, 117; as an element of media coverage, 96, 112, 114–15; endemic and episodic, 97, 114–15; frustrations and, 98–100; imitation and, 96; Unesco conference on media and, 96, 100, 107–8. *See also* Terrorism.

Waltz, Kenneth, 114–15

Washington Post, 47

Wedell, George, 79–80, 82, 97

Zambia, 51, 56, 73

Zimbabwe, 15, 16 n.1, 39 n.1, 51, 56

Zimbabwe *Herald*, 43–44, 48, 60, 61 nn.5, 6

About the Author

WILLIAM H. MEYER is an Assistant Professor of Political Science at the University of Delaware. He has published articles dealing with international communications and cultural relations in *International Interactions* and *Social Science Quarterly*.